THE BLESSED TRINITY
AND THE SACRAMENTS

THE BLESSED TRINITY
AND THE SACRAMENTS

BY

TAYMANS d'EYPERNON, S.J.

Professor of Theology at the University of Louvain

OS JUSTI
PRESS

LINCOLN, NEBRASKA

This Edition 1961

Library of Congress Catalog. Card No. 60-14821.

This book is a translation of LA SAINTE TRINITE ET LES SACREMENTS
published by Desclée de Brouwer, Paris.

MADE AND PRINTED IN THE REPUBLIC OF IRELAND BY CAHILL AND
CO. LTD., FOR CLONMORE AND REYNOLDS LTD. NIHIL OBSTAT :
IOANNES O'DONOGHUE, CENSOR DEPUT. IMPRIMI POTEST :
✠ IOANNES CAROLUS, ARCHIEP. DUBLINEN., HIBERNIAE PRIMAS.
DUBLINI, I FEB. 1960.

CONTENTS

INTRODUCTION

THOUGH the sacraments are not everything in the life of man, they have, nevertheless, a vitally essential rôle to play. "Unless a man be born again of water and the Holy Ghost", said Christ, "he cannot enter the kingdom of heaven."[1] It is important, then, to establish what exactly is the place of the sacraments in life, and to do this we must first recall what a sacrament is.

It is not our intention to retrace the history of the word "sacramentum", a subject already treated authoritatively in several theological works[2]; nor shall we trace back to its origins the definition of a sacrament reached by the Church after centuries of theological research[3]. We wish, rather, to examine the content of this definition that it may yield a deeper appreciation of the sacramental rites and become a source of strength and inspiration for the Christian of to-day.

The Church tells us that the sacraments are efficacious signs of grace These few words, which express the mystery of our divinization by grace, demand that we make an effort to penetrate their meaning. The sacraments are signs. Origen says[4] that a sign is a visible thing that evokes the idea of something invisible. St. Augustine, proceeding from the same point of view, explains in his sermon that we call them sacraments "because in them we see one thing and recognize another. What is seen has a corporeal appearance; what is recognized is a spiritual fruit"[5]. These explanations, however, raise further problems: What does a sacrament signify? What is the invisible reality that it symbolizes? What is the spiritual fruit that one must recognize in the visible element?

---

[1] John, III, 5.
[2] Among others, Fr. Jos. de Ghellinck's *Pour l'Histoire du mot Sacramentum*, Spicilegium, 1924.
[3] Cf. Pourrat: *La Théologie Sacramentaire*, Chapter 1; *Dict. de Théol. Cath.*, *Sacramentum*.
[4] In Epist ad Rom., IV, 2; P.G., XIV, 968.
[5] *Sermones*, 272; P.L. XXXVIII, 1247.

Obviously it is not enough to say that a sacrament, like every other visible creature, reveals the invisible God Who made it. Undoubtedly the material universe affords the revelation of God. But the sacraments are not part of the order of natural creation; they belong to the order of grace which goes further than revealing God merely as Creator. Grace includes an invitation from God as Our Saviour to avail ourselves of the treasures hidden in His life. Viewed in this light, the sacraments appear as signs in a new sense. In their lowly and complex sense-perceptible reality, they are, by virtue of the supernatural order to which they belong, so many revelations of the inner life of God.

If, however, the sacraments were no more than mere signs, signs admittedly of God as Saviour, Who invites us into the intimacy of His personal mystery, they would be confined to the order of intention only and would not possess the effective power of transforming men divinely. But this is precisely one of the domains in which Christianity transcends all other religions. The latter are limited to influencing the moral and psychological powers of man; Christianity affects first and foremost the deepest recesses of man's being whence its influence extends to the whole range of man's actions.

Baptism is a real birth. Penance really restores life to the repentant sinner. As sacraments, they are not only signs of grace, they effectively cause grace in the soul. They sanctify man, body and soul, reaching the depths of the soul through the channel of the body. This truth is enshrined in tradition and is based ultimately on the Incarnation of the Word. According to the beautiful expression of St. Augustine, the Body of Our Saviour Himself is a sacrament "in a certain sense"[6].

Tertullian had already expressed the same truth in words of astonishing realism. "The body", he says, "is the pivot of salvation. For when the soul is united with God it is the body which makes the union possible. The body is washed that the soul may be purified; the body is anointed that the soul may be consecrated; the body is sealed that the soul may be strengthened. In the imposition of hands, the body is overshadowed that the soul may

---

[6] " Sicut ergo secundum quemdam modum, sacramentum corporis Christi; corpus Christi est". (*Epistulae*, XCVIII, 9; *P. L.*, XXXIII, 364.)

be illumined by the Spirit; the body is fed with the Body and Blood of Christ that the soul may be nourished with God"[7].

A century later, St. Cyril of Jerusalem repeats this theme of the Spirit sanctifying the soul through the body: "Water is poured over the exterior and the Spirit cleanses the soul interiorly. . . . If fire passing through the dense substance of iron transforms it wholly into fire, what wonder that the Spirit should pass into the depths of the soul?"[8].

Speaking of Confirmation, St. Cyril makes a bold comparison between that sacrament and the Blessed Eucharist, and in striking language he expresses the reality of God's coming into the soul:

"Just as the Eucharistic Bread, after the invocation of the Spirit, is no longer ordinary bread but the Body of Christ, so this unction is no longer a mere natural anointing; it is the gift of Christ and of the Holy Spirit by the presence of Whose divinity it is rendered (supernaturally) effective"[9].

This truth is repeated by all the Fathers who treat this subject, and all, even the Alexandrians who insist so much on the sacraments as signs, give witness in their writings to the doctrine of the supernatural causality of the sacraments. St. Augustine gives perfect expression to the common doctrine when he writes of Baptism:

"Thus, water, by exteriorly manifesting the bestowal of grace and of the Holy Spirit, effectively bestows that grace interiorly and by it man who was born of Adam is born to newness of life in Christ"[10].

---

[7] "Caro salutis est cardo. De qua cum anima Deo alligatur ipsa est quae efficit ut anima alligari possit. Scilicet, caro abluitur ut anima mundetur; caro ungitur, ut anima consecretur; caro signatur ut anima muniatur; caro manus impositione adumbratur, ut et anima spiritu illuminetur; caro corpore et sanguine Christi vescitur ut et anima de Deo saginetur." (*De Carnis Resurrectione*, 8, *P.L.*, II, 806).

[8] "Aqua exterius circumfunditur, Spiritus et interius animam abluit absque defectu. Et quid miraris? Sume exemplum corporeum, parvum quidem et humile, utile autem simpliciorbus. Si ignis per crassitudinem ferri transiens, intra totam rem efficit ignem. . . . Quid miraris si Spiritus Sanctus in intima animae ingreditur?" (*Catecheses*, XVII, 14; *P.G.*, XXXV, 985).

[9] "Nam sicut panis eucharistiae post invocationem Sancti Spiritus non est communis panis, sed corpus Christi, ita et sanctum istud unguentum non amplius nudum neque, si quis ita appellare malit, commune unguentum est post invocationem, sed Christi donarium et Spiritus Sancti, presentia divinitatis eius efficiens factum, quod quidem symbolice fronti aliisque sensibus tuis illinitur; ac dum unguento visibili inungitur corpus, sancto et vivifico spiritu anima sanctificatur." (*Cateches.* XC XXI (Myst. 3), 3; *P.G.*, XXXV, 1089.)

[10] "Aqua igitur exhibens forinsecus beneficium gratiae, et Spiritus operans intrinsecus beneficium gratiae . . . regenerant hominem in uno Christo ex uno Adamo generatum." (*Epistulae*, XCVIII (*Bonifacio*), 2; *P.L.*, XXXIII, 360.)

Here we have expressed the deep and penetrating action of God, Who through the instrumentality of material elements firstly sanctifies the deep recesses of man's being, and thence spreads His sanctifying influence over man's actions.

Material or sense-perceptible elements, raised by grace to the rank of sacraments, become the channel of God's presence and implant in man's soul a "fountain springing up into eternal life". The sacraments are truly *efficacious* signs of grace. But the Divine Presence effected by the sacraments—and this is the central point of the present study—is not just the presence of the Divine Nature or of One Divine Person. It is the presence of the Three Persons of the Blessed Trinity.

In speaking of the Divine Life born and nourished in us by the sacraments, it is to be remembered that the Life of God is the Life of Three Persons. The Divine Life we receive by grace is the personal Divine Life of the Three Persons of the Trinity.

Necessarily, then, the Three Persons are active in each of the sacraments, disposing us to receive their Presence, assimilating our life to Theirs, and enabling us to grow continually in grace.

On this point tradition is quite explicit. When they write of the action of God in and through the sacraments, the Fathers and ecclesiastical writers refer to the indwelling of the Blessed Trinity in us. They teach that the root and foundation of our sanctification is the Life of the Blessed Three, a Life that is supremely personal and supremely social, personal and social on the divine plane.

Sometimes the power of transforming the material element into a source of grace is attributed to the Word of Christ, as in St. Augustine's *"Detrahe verbum et quid est aqua nisi aqua?"*[11] At other times the mysterious power of renewing the human heart is attributed to the Holy Ghost Who sanctifies the water or the chrism.

"If there is grace in the baptismal water", says St. Basil, "it does not derive from the nature of the water itself, but from the presence of the Holy Spirit"[12].

Elsewhere the life of grace is said to be the work of the Father and of the Son[13].

---

[11] *In Joannnis Evangelium*, tr. LXXX, 3; P.L. XXXV, 1840.

[12] *De Spiritu Sancto*, XV, 35; P.G., XXXIV, 131.

[13] Cf. St. Ambrose: " Neque enim humanae opis est divina conficere, sed tuum Domine munus et Patris est." (*De Spir. Sancto*, Prologus, n. 18; P.L., XVI, 708.)

Finally, the sanctification of men and of things is sometimes attributed to the Blessed Trinity. St. John Chrysostom says:

"Neither angel nor archangel can accomplish anything in the gifts of God; the Father and the Son and the Holy Ghost dispose of everything. The priest but lends his lips and his hands"[14].

From this it is clear that the Fathers of the Church, following the law of attribution, at various times assign the work of our sanctification to the Son, or to the Holy Ghost, or to the Father and Son, while elsewhere they recognize it as the common operation of the Blessed Trinity. The presence and operation of the Three Divine Persons is more emphatically underlined when the Fathers treat of the baptismal formula.

"Perhaps you may enquire," says Origen, "why St. Paul in speaking of Baptism mentions Christ alone—*Baptizati sumus in Christo*—whereas Christ commanded the disciples to baptise all peoples in the Name of the Father and of the Son and of the Holy Ghost, and there is no real baptism but by the invocation of the Trinity?"[15].

From his manner of posing the question one can divine the trend of the author's thought. Baptism in Christ cannot mean the exclusive action of one Divine Person in the sanctification of a Christian. Origen's thought becomes much more explicit when he answers the question. He says that St. Paul wished to insist on the Christian's participation in the Death and Resurrection of Christ.

Could one imagine his saying, "We who are baptised in the Father and the Holy Ghost are baptized in their Death and Resurrection"? Here, as often elsewhere in quoting the Scriptures, St. Paul is content to use extracts that will emphasize the particular truth he is teaching; he does not always cite the complete text[16].

St. Cyprian is astonished that some Christians should maintain the validity of a Baptism conferred solely in the Name of Christ.

---

[14] "Neque angelus neque archangelus in iis quae a Deo data sunt aliquid efficere potest, sed Pater et Filius et Spiritus Sanctus omnia administat; Sacerdos vero linguam suam commodat manum porrigit." (*In Joann. homil.*, LXXXVI, 4; P.G., LXI, 472.)

[15] "Requiras fortasse etiam hoc quod cum ipse Dominus dixerit ad discipulos ut baptizarent omnes gentes in nomine Patris et Filii et Spiritus Sancti, cur hic Apostolus solius Christi in baptismo nomen assumpserit dicens, *Quicumque baptizati sumus in Christo,* cum utique non habeatur legitimum baptisma nisi sub nomine Trinitatis." (*In Rom. Comment.*, V., 8; P.G., XIV, 1039, 1040).

[16] ibid.

How can this be possible, he says, since Christ Himself has commanded us to baptize in the Name of the whole Trinity—*in plena et adunata Trinitate?*[17].

For St. Hilary the important consideration is that the Father, Son and Holy Ghost, being the one indivisible principle of all things, must also necessarily be the one principle of all grace:

"For there is but one author of all things: one Father from whom all things originate; one Only Begotten by Whom all things exist; and one Spirit, the gift (of God) in all things. . . . Nor can anything be wanting to this divine economy, since in the Father, Son and Holy Ghost there are united infinity in the Eternal, beauty in the Image, and joy in the Gift"[18].

The thesis of St. Hilary is very precise. There is no other divine causality except that which originates from the Father, by the Son, in the Holy Ghost and which alone is the cause of all beauty and beatitude. Consequently our adoption as sons of God is caused by the whole Trinity sanctifying us.

There is a wealth of testimony that could be adduced from the writings of the Fathers. St. Basil, for example, in his *De Spiritu Sancto*[19], gives an exegesis of the baptismal formula, drawing on texts that are found in St. Irenaeus: the Father anoints, the Son is the Anointed, and the Holy Ghost is the Unction.

St. Gregory Nazianzen, also commenting on the formula, reiterates his thesis that the revelation of God took place in three stages: the Father was known in the Old Testament, the Son manifests Himself to us in the New, and the Holy Ghost abides in the Church since the Ascension of our Lord. Hence the perfect Baptism is that which omits none of the Divine Persons[20]. St. Ambrose might be cited on the same theme[21].

But the following text from St. Jerome seems to us more profoundly illuminating, for it stresses that the unity of God's external operation derives from the Trinity of Persons in God. There can

[17] *Epistulae*, LXXIII, 18; *P.L.*, III, 1120.

[18] " Auctor unus est omnium; unus est enim Deus Pater ex quo omnia; et unus unigenitus Dominus Noster Jesus Christus per quem omnia; et unus Spiritus donum in omnibus. Omnia ergo sunt suis virtutibus et meritus ordinata; una potestas ex quo omnia, una progenies per quem omnia; perfectae spei munus unum. Nec deesse quidquam consummationi tantae reperietur, intra quam sit in Patre et Filio et Spiritu Sancto, infinitas in aeterno, species in imagine, usus in munere." (*De Trinitate*, II, 1; *P.L.*, X, 50).

[19] XII, 28; *P.G.*, XXXIV, 116.

[20] *Orationes*, XXXIII, 17; *P.G.*, XXXVIII, 236.

[21] *De Spiritu Sancto*, I, 3, 42; *P.L.*, XVI, 714.

be no unity which does not originate in the Trinity; and all unity bears a relation to its triune origin:

"There is one Lord and one God, because the overlordship of the Father and of the Son is one Divinity. It is on this account, too, that our faith is one, since we believe in the Father and in the Son and in the Holy Ghost. In the same way, Baptism is one, for we are baptized in the Father and in the Son and in the Holy Ghost. We are thrice immersed in the water to express that this one vivifying sacrament is the work of the whole Trinity"[22].

The presence and action of the Blessed Trinity in the sacraments has as its effect an adaptation of the Christian to the personal Life of the Divine Persons; we receive the Divine Persons within us as the highest gift of God to man. Let us dwell a little on this sublime truth.

Theology teaches that the sacraments are the work of Christ. How then can we speak of them as channels of the action of the whole Trinity?

When we maintain that the Father, Son and Holy Ghost are active in every sacrament are we merely using emphatic language to express the Divine causality?

Is it not an unwarranted exaggeration of the domain of sacramental efficiency to assert that the Sacraments must be viewed in relation to the Trinity and to maintain that the end of every sacrament consists in establishing a certain conformity between the Christian and the life of the Divine Persons within the Trinity?

The answer to these questions will emerge if we consider Who it is Who acts in Christ. Undoubtedly it is in virtue of His Sacred Humanity that Christ, God made Man, exercises the power to sanctify the members of His Mystical Body. The sacraments are an extension of this sanctifying power of the Humanity of Christ. But every act of a personal agent must always be attributed to the person as its author. Hence every act of Christ is an act of His Divine Person, the Unique Word of God. Since in Christ there is but One Person, we can say with truth, "God wept; God suffered; God died for us".

---

[22] " Unus est Dominus et unus est Deus, quia Patris et Filii dominatio una divinitas est. Propterea et fides una dicitur quia similiter in Patrem et in Filium et in Spiritum Sanctum credimus. Et baptisma unum; eodem enim modo et in Patrem et in Filium et in Spiritum Sanctum baptizamur. Et ter mergimur, ut Trinitatis unum efficax appareat sacramentum ". (*In Epistulam ad Ephes.* Comment, 2, 4, 5; *P.L.*, XXVI, 496).

Similarly the miracles which Christ worked were not performed by some power other than the power of Christ. He worked miracles by His Own power, by the Divine power of the Word. So too in the sacraments, in which Christ continues His miracles of healing and of resurrection, it is the Word Who is active, reaching deep into souls through the ministry of material elements; and in every sacrament, by the divinizing power of grace, the Word brings the life of man into closer conformity with His Own Divine Life in the bosom of the Father.

Now whatever is done by One Divine Person in our created world, is also done by the other Divine Persons, each acting in the manner proper to His Own Divine Personality. In all the works of God we must always recognize the unity of operation common to the Three Divine Persons.

In the work of Redemption, the Father and the Holy Ghost are, with the Son, the cause of our salvation, but not in the same way. The Son alone became Man, was born, suffered, died and rose again from the dead. But He would not have done any of these things had He not been sent by the Father; nor would His mission have been completed had He not, with the Father, sent the Holy Ghost Who, as the Spirit of love and of holiness, brings every work of God to its crowning perfection.

It follows, then, that our salvation is in the strictest sense an operation of the Blessed Trinity. The Three Divine Persons are together the author of salvation; the one act of redemption is realized by the Father, Son and Holy Ghost; salvation is a personal gift made by each of the Divine Persons.

This being true of salvation as a whole, we need not hesitate to recognize the same mode of operation in the prolongation of the redemptive action, that is, in the application of the fruits of the Redemption. We shall see the sacraments not only as the prolongation of Christ's action on earth; in them we shall see the action of the Word in Person, and with that of the Word, the action of the Father and of the Holy Ghost.

Christ is the centre of the whole redemptive system, but in and through Christ there is everywhere an echo of the Trinity. Each sacrament has as its purpose to bring man into greater conformity with the Son, and through Him to a closer assimilation to the Blessed Trinity in Its inner life. The sacraments, each in its own particular way, express different aspects of the Divine plan to wed time and eternity, enabling Christians to reproduce in their lives a reflex of the eternal mystery of God.

This, then, is the reason why God in His love has stooped so low to us. It is in a material universe that our destiny is shaped and shattered and remade. The material world is a vast plain of battle, scarred with the marks of our defeat, or resplendent with the trophies of victory. Matter is man's strength and his weakness, for it is by his life amid material things and by his use of them that man rises above himself; and on the other hand, it is the material part of our nature that bleeds and is broken in the press of life.

It was divinely fitting that God should come and apply His saving Omnipotence to this essential part of His creation, the most vulnerable of all. He does this by the sacraments. They not only are signs of His coming, they actually contain the divine healing power and apply it to our souls.

In them matter is elevated to the rank of a bond between God and man and a symbol of the infinite mystery of God's love; raised to sacramental dignity, matter is not only the channel by which the thought and prayer of the creature rise to the Uncreated, but the channel by which God Himself really comes to His creatures to dwell in them forever. *Et mansionem apud eum faciemus*[23].

---

[23] John, XIV, 23.

Note: The present work was finished before the author received the excellent book by Père Philippon, O.P., *Les Sacrements dans la vie chrétienne*, (Bruges: Desclée de Brouwer, 1946). The author regrets that he was unable to quote from Père Philippon's work.

CHAPTER I

EFFECTS OF THE SACRAMENTS :

GRACE AND CHARACTER

IF WE ARE to understand the rôle of the sacraments in the Christian life we must be prepared to face certain problems, one of which appears at first sight almost insoluble. A sacrament can be valid, that is, possess all the elements required for its existence as a sacrament, and yet fail to produce grace, because of some obstacle opposed to it by the soul [1].

How can we solve this enigma? Of itself a sacrament ought to produce grace. By definition, it is a *signum efficax gratiae*. If for extrinsic reasons a sacrament does not confer grace, what does it confer? Does it produce any effect whatsoever in the soul? If it produces no effect, can it truly be called a sacrament? Does it not seem contradictory to speak of a cause that does not exercise causality?

These questions could not be ignored by the Christian conscience, and the efforts of theologians to find a satisfactory answer to them have opened up vast perspectives in the domain of sacramental theology.

The first traces of a solution derive from the teaching of Peter Lombard in the 12th century. The following is a brief resumé of the line of argument adopted:

The sacraments, which normally should produce grace, do not in fact produce it when the subject is not properly disposed. Three sacraments, however—Baptism, Confirmation and Holy Orders—always confer an indelible character, even on a subject

---

[1] The obstacle referred to here is what theologians call an *obex ad fructum sacramenti* and consists in the lack of the requisite disposition in the soul of the recipient; the defective disposition may be either formal—when it is conscious and deliberate—or material, as when the recipient is unaware of the defect. The latter would take place in the case of a sinner who goes to confession not knowing that supernatural attrition is required for the remission of sin.

who is not properly disposed. Hence, provided that the conditions for validity are fulfilled, these sacraments always produce an effect, namely, a sacramental character.

Using the law of analogy, may one not venture to suggest that the other sacraments also possess the power of imprinting some mark on the soul? Obviously this mark would not be an indelible sacramental character; nor could it be sanctifying grace, which is excluded on the hypothesis of the subject being improperly disposed. The seal or mark conferred would be rather a claim to grace, and as soon as the obstacle to the reception of grace is removed the soul would receive sacramental grace in virtue of the mark imprinted by the sacrament.

To elucidate this theory theologians had recourse to the famous distinction between the sacramental sign together with the effect always produced by a valid sacrament (*sacramentum et res*), and sanctifying grace (*res tantum*) which is received only if the soul does not oppose an obstacle to its reception. Using this distinction, theologians maintained that the effect which was always produced was, in the case of Baptism, Confirmation and Holy Orders, the sacramental character, and in the case of the other sacraments an *ornatus animae,* an embellishment of the soul which primarily entailed a claim to the subsequent reception of grace once the obstacle was removed.

From the above-mentioned distinction there arose in the 13th century an explanation of the mode of sacramental causality which is associated with the name of Alexander of Hales. If he was not its author, he was at least an ardent supporter of what is known as dispositive causality.

According to this theory, the soul is always enriched by the reception of any sacrament, at least by receiving this gift or mark or seal which *disposes* the soul to receive grace and in virtue of which God cannot but infuse grace once the obstacle is removed. The importance and lasting success of this theory can be judged from the fact that to-day theologians admit *reviviscentia gratiae* in the case of all the sacraments except the Blessed Eucharist [2].

---

[2] It is hard to see why the Blessed Eucharist should be made an exception. The reason commonly adduced is that once the Species are consumed there remains nothing of the sacrament; hence it is impossible to see how the sacrament could be " revived ". This reasoning, however, might equally be applied to the other sacraments, for there remains nothing of the sacraments of Baptism and Penance when the pouring of the water or the pronouncement of the words of absolution has been completed.

It is not surprising that the theory of dispositive causality, abandoned after the Council of Trent, has at the present time found a new lease of life under a new form. If sanctifying grace, which was impeded from vivifying the soul at the reception of a sacrament, can return after the removal of the obstacle, must we not admit that the sacrament did in fact confer some seed, as it were, of divine life; or, to speak the language of dispositive causality, can we not say that the sacrament implanted an exigence of grace, a claim to the subsequent reception of grace?

Theological writers deliberately refrain from attempting to give a precise statement of the nature of this claim to grace, which is so potent that in some sort it constrains God to infuse grace once the subject is properly disposed. Even if we admit the theory of intentional causality, so brilliantly proposed by Cardinal Billot as a development from the theory of dispositive causality, there remains the impression of a *deus ex machina* very opportunely introduced to explain the reviviscence of grace.

We are still ignorant of the exact nature of the mark or trace left in the soul by the reception of every sacrament. There is room here for a further advance in the domain of sacramental theology, and we are convinced that this advance will be made by taking greater account of the action of the Blessed Trinity in the soul of the adopted children of God and by striving after a better understanding of the rôle of the sacraments in establishing and nourishing the life of the Blessed Trinity within us. Let us follow this line of thought a little further.

Our primary concern in life is to be born, grow up and reach fulfilment as sons of God. This is the very essence of the supernatural life. Is it not, then, to be expected that the Divine Life in us, our participation as sons in the Life of the Father, should reproduce in our contingent existence and in a contingent way (*secundum mensuram gratiae*) something of the absolute and necessary relations that exist in the Blessed Trinity?

God exists as Three Divine Persons in the absolute unity of the Divine Nature; we exist supernaturally by participating through sanctifying grace in the Life of the same Three Divine Persons. Our adoptive sonship of God is a relation of conformity with the Eternal Son and includes a true generation by the Father, a real assimilation to the Son and an outpouring of the Holy Ghost.

This is the sublime effect of sanctifying grace in us and it is made possible only by the consummating action of the Spirit of Love in our souls.

Why did the Saviour lay such emphasis on the promise of the Paraclete? Because supernatural life is not merely a relation to the Father and the Son; the Father and the Son dwell in their creatures uniquely in and through the Holy Ghost.

Nor is this difficult to understand. The Father and the Son expressed their love in every divine action. The expression of the mutual love of the Father and the Son within the eternal Godhead is an infinite surge of love whence proceeds the Holy Ghost; the external expression of their love in creation is a mission of the Holy Ghost. In the plan of the Father and Son to sanctify creatures there is included an outpouring of the Holy Spirit. It is for this reason that charity is inherent in the state of grace, since charity consists in abiding in the love of God, that is, in the Holy Ghost.

Before applying these principles to the sacramental system, and more especially to the problem of "reviviscence", it is well to be sure that such was from the beginning the accepted view of sanctifying grace. The phrase in which St. Paul reminds the Corinthians that they are the temple of the Holy Ghost [3] was explained by the Fathers in terms that left no doubt that the sanctification of the human soul was the special operation of the Holy Ghost.

St. Cyril of Alexandria is not the only one to insist on the vivifying and sanctifying action of the Holy Spirit; the whole tradition of the Greek Fathers is of the same mind and it is echoed among the Latins by St. Hilary [4], St. Ambrose [5] and St. Augustine [6]. The examination of a few patristic texts will enable us to appreciate the thought of the early Christian centuries in all its authenticity.

St. Irenaeus who used the varied resources of figurative expression to underline the action of the Three Divine Persons in the works of God does not hesitate to attribute the sanctification of the faithful to the Holy Spirit. It is He Who effects the transformation of the old man of sin into the new man of grace.

"Just as the wild olive after grafting does not lose its nature as

---

[3] I. Cor. VI, 19.
[4] *De Trinitate*, VIII, 21; *P.L.*, X, 252.
[5] *De Spiritu Sancto*, I, 6, 77; *P.L.*, XVI, 723.
[6] *De Trinitate*, XV, 26, 46; *P.L.*, XLII, 1093.

a tree but produces a different kind of fruit and is called by a new name . . . so man, by receiving the Holy Ghost, does not lose his carnal nature, but by his acts he produces fruits of a new kind and receives a new name to express his transformation and elevation. For he is now called not just flesh and blood, but the 'spiritual man' " [7].

The same thought is found in the Syrian writer Aphraates:

"All those who are born of the flesh are deprived of the Spirit until they approach the waters of regeneration. At Baptism they receive the Holy Ghost. At their first birth they receive an 'animal spirit', which is indeed immortal, as it is written: *factus est homo in animam viventem* (Gen. II, 7). By the second birth of Baptism man receives the holy and immortal Spirit as the gift of the Godhead . . . If a man grieves the Spirit he received in Baptism, the Spirit leaves him before his death and returns to Christ and accuses the man who has grieved Him" [8].

This quotation from Aphraates contains a thought dear to the heart of St. Irenaeus: the spiritual man is generated at Baptism by receiving a new form which binds him to Christ, and this form is the presence of the Holy Ghost.

The thought of St. Athanasius is much more precise. His theology is everywhere dominated by the mystery of the Trinity. Writing against the Arians, his primary aim was to convince them of the difference between the Only Begotten Son and the adoptive sons of God.

"We are not", he says, "in the Father in the same way in which the Son is in the Father. For the Son does not need to participate in the Spirit nor to receive the Spirit in order that He may abide in the Father; on the contary, it is the Son Who bestows the spirit

---

[7] "Quemadmodum oleaster inserta substantiam quidem ligni non amittit, qualitatem autem fructus immutat et aliud percipit vocabulum, jam non oleaster sed fructifera oliva existens edicitur; sic et homo per fidem insertus et assumens Spiritum Dei, substantiam quidem carnis non amittit, qualitatem autem fructus operum immutat et aliud accipit vocabulum, significans illam quae in melius est transmutationem. Jam non caro et sanguis, sed homo spiritalis existens edicitur." (*Adv. Haer.*, V, 10; *P.G.*, VII, 1148).

[8] Ab omnibus enim de corpore natis Spiritus abest donec ad aquae regenerationem accedant; tunc accipiunt Spiritum Sanctum. In priori quidem generatione nascuntur spiritu animali praediti qui in homine creatur nec morietur unquam, sicut scriptum est: *Factum est homo in animam viventem* (Gen. II, 7). At in altera, baptismi scilicet regeneratione, Spiritum Sanctum ex ipsa divinitate recipiunt immortalem . . . Ex homine autem qui Spiritum ex aqua receptum contristavit, egreditur Spiritus priusquam ille moriatur atque . . . ad Christum vadens, hominem accusat a quo contristatus est.' (*Demonstrat.*, VI, 14; *Patrol. Syr.*, I, 291).

on all men. Similarly it is not the Spirit Who unites the Word to the Father; rather the Spirit receives this from the Word. Finally, the Son is in the Father as His Image and the splendour of His substance; we, however, remain strangers and at a distance from God unless the Spirit dwells in us" [9].

Having made this distinction, Athanasius goes on to describe the action of the Holy Ghost in us:

"By participating in the Spirit we are united to the Godhead Itself. Accordingly, our abiding in the Father is not the result of our own effort but of the action of the Spirit Who is in us and Who abides in us as long as we cherish Him by our profession of faith" [10].

Accordingly, while the Son is Son by the fact of His generation from the Father, independently of the Holy Ghost, we, the adopted sons of God, live in union with the Father only by participating in the Holy Ghost. The grace that transforms a sinner into a son of God is always a mission of the Holy Ghost.

In the same line of thought we find the following words of St. Cyril of Jerusalem:

"If your piety is sincere, the Holy Ghost descends on you and the voice of the Father is heard from on high saying, not 'This is My Son', but 'This person has become My son' " [11].

St. Basil attributes the graces and virtues that adorn the sanctified soul to the Holy Ghost:

"The Spirit shines in the soul of those who are purified of all stain and by their communion with Him He gives them spiritual existence. Just as brilliant and translucent bodies, penetrated by the rays of the sun, gleam with additional splendour and in their turn radiate a more intense brilliance, so those souls that are the temples

---

[9] " Non igitur ut est Filius in Patre, ita et nos in Patre sumus. Namque Filius non fit Spiritu particeps ut sit in Patre, neque ipse Spiritum accipit, sed eum potius omnibus impertit.   Nec item Spiritus Verbum cum Patre conjungit, sed potius Spiritus hoc a Verbo accipit.   Denique Filius in Patre est tanquam proprium eius Verbum et splendor; nos autem siquidem absit Spiritus alieni et procul a Deo sumus." (*Adv. Arianos Orationes*, III, 24; P.C., XXVIII, 373).

[10] " Sed Spiritus participes effecti, cum ipsa conjungimur divinitate, ac proinde, non nostrum est nos esse in Patre sed Spiritus qui in nobis est et in nobis manet quamdiu scilicet eum in nobis confessione servamus." (*ibid.*).

[11] " Si et tu habeas sinceram pietatem, descendit in te Spiritus Sanctus et vox Paterna tibi desuper resonat; non, hic est Filius meus; sed, *hic factus est filius meus.*" (*Catechese*, III, 14; P.G. XXXV, 444).

of the Spirit are bathed in His light and become spiritual and radiate grace to others" [12].

St. Cyril of Alexandria repeatedly stresses the rôle of the Holy Spirit in the sanctification of the soul. Let it suffice to quote the basic argument he uses both in refuting his adversaries and in strengthening the faithful in their practice of the Christian life: "If the Holy Spirit is not really God, why does the Scripture say that we must be born of the Spirit in order to be born of God?" [13]

The repeated testimony of the early centuries, which we have very briefly sketched, throws a revealing light on the problem of the sacraments. A sacrament is an efficacious sign of grace. Of itself it tends to the justification of the sinner and to growth in Divine Life and friendship with God. This is possible only in and through the Holy Ghost.

One cannot live in the Father and in the Son unless one possesses the Spirit of the Father and the Son. The Father and the Son take up their abode in our souls only through the Holy Ghost. We can see something of a parallel in the natural human family, where the birth of a child helps to establish a higher degree of mutual understanding and love which we call the family spirit.

What happens if the Holy Spirit is excluded from the soul of a person who receives a sacrament in unworthy dispositions? Since such a person rejects charity he also rejects the Holy Ghost and cannot receive sanctifying grace.

Such a person is the term of a divine action, a supernatural action which, nevertheless, does not include the indwelling of the Blessed Trinity in the soul. How can this action be defined?

The function of the sacraments is to inaugurate, develop and bring to perfection our adoptive sonship of God. This sonship implies two things—conformity with Christ and a life of love in the Spirit. Without these two elements, sonship of God is inconceivable. The Father and the Son and the Holy Ghost come and dwell in our souls only when they recognize in us a resemblance to the Son. Secondly, by his likeness to the Son, man is committed to

---

[12] " Hic (Spiritus) iis qui ab omni sorde purgati sunt illucescens, per communionem quam cum ipso habent spirituales reduit. Et quemadmodum corpora nitida pellucidaque contacta radio fiunt et ipsa supra modum splendida, et alium fulgorem ex sese profundunt, ita animae quae Spiritum ferunt illustranturque a Spiritu, fiunt et ipsae spirituales et in alios gratiam emittunt." *De Spiritu Sancto*, IX, 22/23; *P.G.*, XXXII, 109).

[13] Cf. *In joannem Commentarius*, 1, 9 (1, 13); *P.G.*, LXXV, 157; et alibi.

a life of love in the Spirit, and once he accepts this life of divine charity, the Father and the Son send him the Spirit of love, the Holy Ghost.

This process takes place unhindered at the Baptism of an infant. In the case of an adult who opposes an obstacle to the reception of the Holy Ghost, he still receives, in virtue of the sacrament, a stamp or seal of likeness to the Son. Even though the Three Divine Persons are not received into the soul, they leave a mark of resemblance to the Son.

Such a Christian might be called still-born rather than re-born. A still-born baby, even though it lacks life, is none the less an existing reality; it is the term of an act of generation, and one can recognise in such a baby a likeness to its parents and a resemblance to its brothers and sisters. In some such way a Christian who though called to divine sonship refuses to accept the conditions of the Divine Life, bears some resemblance to Christ, but he does not live in Christ. He is a still-born Christian.

In our view, the *ornatus animae* proposed by the theory of dispositive causality would consist in a resemblance to Christ which is produced by all the sacraments in varying degrees. It is imprinted in indelible fashion by three sacraments and is called the sacramental character; but the other sacraments also cause a real if transitory likeness to Christ, as impermanent as the changes in facial expression that come and go with the ever-changing rhythm of existence.

It is our contention that each sacrament, in its own way and according to its own proper end and the grace it is destined to produce, causes a likeness between the adopted son of God and the Eternal Son, between the members and the Head of the Mystical Body.

Baptism, the sacrament of supernatural birth, is essentially a generation by the Eternal Father to the image of the unique Prototype—the Son. By it we are reborn in time in conformity with Him Who is eternally born in the bosom of the Father.

Confirmation commissions us for the work of reconstructing the world and gives us the likeness of Christ in His rôle as Artisan of our salvation. No effort of ours can bear fruit unless it is assimilated to the redemptive effort of the Son.

Penance gives us a share in the strength of the Saviour in His combat with evil and a determination to destroy sin in ourselves and replace it by His divine life . . . *ut vitam habeant et abundantius habeant.* Our spiritual rehabilitation by the sacrament of Penance is figured in the miraculous cures wrought by Christ while on earth.

Extreme Unction assimilates us to the dying Christ, so that in union with Him and by conformity between our death and His our supreme offering of ourselves may be consummated in Him.

Holy Orders makes us priests sharing in the Priesthood of the unique High-Priest Who alone achieves the reconciliation of all things with the Father.

Matrimony, according to the teaching of St. Paul, effects a real conformity between the wedded love of man and woman and the mystery of Christ ever loving His Church and sharing His life with her.

The Blessed Eucharist, finally, brings our likeness with the Son to the highest degree possible on earth, since It both signifies and produces a transforming union of the Christian in Christ [14].

The resemblance to the Son caused in us by the sacraments includes a claim to grace. As a father, seeing his own resemblance in the features of his child and finding in that likeness an appeal to his paternity, is inspired to love and benevolence, so God the Father, recognizing in us the image of His Only Begotten inclines towards us with ineffable love. Without any doubt the resemblance to Christ caused by the sacraments should issue in sanctifying grace: but it is in itself distinct from sanctifying grace.

A child, in spite of his resemblance to his parents, may refuse to respond to their love, may separate himself from them and may reject the spirit of his family. Similarly a Christian, even though stamped with the traits of Christ, may refuse to live in Christ and in His Father, by refusing to live in the Holy Spirit and by excluding charity from his heart.

It would appear that this position is well founded if we consider that a validly conferred sacrament, even if it does not always produce grace, is none the less a real sacrament. A person who is validly baptized but who opposes an obstacle to the reception of grace, if he dies in this state dies as a Christian, signed with the

---

[14] What is briefly indicated here will be developed at greater length when we come to treat each sacrament in turn.

seal of Christ. He dies a Christian because he bears the sacramental character, which is a mark of conformity with Christ; he is not saved because he is not united with Christ by Grace.

A paradox, if you will, but understandable if one remembers that divine generation should reach its final flowering and its normal and necessary development in a life of friendship with Christ. Generation is but the first stage in the process. The full flowering of Divine Life consists in intimate union with God.

From these considerations one can better understand how it is possible for a sacrament to "revive" when in spite of valid reception it has been impeded from immediately producing the grace of friendship. The sacrament, even though it is impeded from causing grace, seals the soul with a mark of quality [15], which resembles a seed which an icy frost prevents from germinating. The unworthiness of the recipient paralyzes the divine action. Once the faulty disposition is amended (*remoto obice*) the inner law of life finds free play and the soul is inundated with divine grace.

It is evident that the sacramental character conferred by Baptism, Confirmation and Holy Orders is distinct from the seal of Christ-likeness common to all the sacraments. Alexander of Hales held that the character was in fact this mark of resemblance to Christ and was a permanent quality inhering in the soul [16] and disposing it for the reception of grace [17]. Regarding the nature of the character, however, we think that the teaching of St. Thomas has not been surpassed, in spite of some recent criticism [18].

For St. Thomas the sacramental character is an active power [19]; it confers a power of doing something. Man does not receive the sacraments for the sole purpose of being healed and sanctified as an individual. The sacraments also depute him for acts of cult. The sacramental character is, therefore, a participation in the priesthood of Christ and "ordains" the recipient to exercise Christian cult; the character confers a mission.

Baptism, for example, renders the Christian apt to participate in the other sacramental rites. Confirmation gives him a mandate to

---

[15] According to scholastic teaching the *ornatus animae* is referred to the category of quality.

[16] He would refer the sacramental character to the category of " *habitus* ".

[17] *S. Th.*, IV, q. VIII, membr. 8.

[18] Cf. Pourrat, *Théologie Sacramentaire, p.* 225.

[19] The character then must be referred to the category of " *potentia* " not of " *habitus* ". Cf. *S. Th.*, III, 63, 2, c.

make public profession of Christ. Holy Orders confers the power to administer the sacraments [20].

If one admits the fundamental thesis of this doctrine, namely, that the character as a participation in the priesthood of Christ always confers a power, one can better grasp why the character, unlike other qualities, is indelible. Whereas it depends on us whether we reject grace and banish the Holy Ghost from our souls, our participation in a divine power depends on God alone and can be annulled or abolished only by Him. Absolutely speaking, God could deprive an unworthy priest of the power of Holy Orders; that He has decided to grant that power irrevocably is known only from revelation.

From our knowledge of this Divine Providence, we can determine why the character, unlike grace and the other divine gifts which we can unfortunately squander, remains intact and inviolable in spite of our sins and infidelities. The reason is that the character is not primarily conferred for the personal life of the member of Christ but in view of the action of that member within the whole Body. The character seals the individual member for the exercise of a particular function as part of the Mystical Body.

It matters little whether one agrees with St. Thomas in his assignation of the powers conferred by the three sacraments which imprint a character; whether Baptism simply disposes us to receive the other sacraments, and whether the character of Confirmation deputes us as witnesses of Christ; what is important, in our view, is the general principle according to which the sacramental character deputes and equips the Christian for the exercise of a public function.

The sacramental character differs from the seal of Christ caused by all the sacraments in that the latter primarily concerns the person who receives the sacrament, whereas the former seals the individual member in view of the function he is called upon to perform towards the whole Body. The character marks the Christian for his social rôle in the Church. The Christian has a double duty to perform: he must live his personal life in super-

---

[20] *Ibid.* art. 4, c.: " Respondeo dicendum quod, sicut dictum est (art. praec.), character est quoddam signaculum, quo anima insignitur ad suscipendum, vel aliis tradendum ea quae sunt divini cultus; divinus autem cultus in quibusdam actionibus consistit; ad actus autem proprie ordinantur potentiae animae sicut essentia ordinatur ad esse; et ideo character non est, sicut in subjecto, in essentia animae, sed in ejus potentia."

natural union with Christ, and, since he forms part of a living organism, he must act on the other members of that organism.

Nor is this social action of the Christian to be regarded merely as the overflow of this personal grace to others; a Christian cannot alienate his personal gifts and graces on the plea that they are his own "surplus". He acts on others by making available to them the common Christian treasury of truth and charity and Divine Life of which Christ is the sole fountainhead.

Even the Christian who has lost sanctifying grace remains capable of making public confession of Christ. By his Baptism he is obliged to do so. The lack of harmony that exists between his personal life and his profession of faith does not prevent him from working for the defence and extension of the Church. He may be lax and tepid in the practice of his religion, but he is capable at times of playing an ardent rôle as a defender of Catholic interests.

The character of Confirmation obliges him to undertake such action. A priest may be unworthy, but by his administration of the sacraments he sheds abroad the riches of grace over the Christian flock.

Undoubtedly there is an obligation on Christians to bring their personal life into harmony with the public function they exercise in the Body of Christ. But in the divine economy of salvation one cannot but admire the Divine Wisdom which does not require that men be as angels in order to receive a mission of which even the angels are unworthy, the mission of working for the increase of the Mystical Body of Christ.

In and beyond the personal destiny of every Christian, God aims at the good and the progress of His Church. Even after he has lost sanctifying grace, a Christian retains the power to act *in aedificationem corporis Christi* [21] for he still retains the sacramental character of Baptism and of Confirmation.

To recapitulate the contents of this chapter: As a result of Christian reflection on the sacraments, there arose a problem that provoked centuries of controversy, namely, the problem of the *sacramentum validum sed informe,* a sacrament that is validly conferred but which fails to produce grace in the soul of the recipient. Linked with this problem was that of the "reviviscence" of grace. It seemed contradictory to speak of a sacrament that re-

---

[21] *Ephesians,* IV, 12.

mained unproductive. Hence theologians tried to discover what was the effect of *every* valid reception of a sacrament.

There was first the theory of the "embellishment of the soul" (*ornatus animae*) a quality inhering in the soul and disposing it for the subsequent reception of grace. But theology was silent on the nature of this *ornatus*.

Patristic tradition, by its insistence on the rôle of the Holy Ghost in the sanctification of the soul, seemed to give an indication of the effect of a valid sacrament which nevertheless did not produce grace. Sanctifying grace, which consists in the regeneration of a soul by the Father in the image of the Son, is conferred only in and through the Holy Ghost. But to every mission of the Holy Ghost there does not always correspond a movement of acceptance on the part of man. To receive Him is to engage oneself to live united to God on terms of reciprocal love.

Let us consider the case of a divine generation which, through man's fault, does not reach this communion in the Spirit, a still-birth, so to speak. Such a generation would seal the soul with a likeness to the Son, a conformity with Christ that includes in itself a claim to grace, yet not the state of grace itself.

In this way the validity of the sacrament is vindicated since it does produce the primary and radical effect of all supernaturalizing action—assimilation to Christ. Thus, too, we can understand how a valid sacrament may fail to produce grace, which is a union of charity in the Holy Ghost.

Finally, we are enabled to distinguish between the sacramental character and the configuration with Christ that is common to all the sacraments. The character is indeed a configuration with Christ, but it consists specifically in a participation in the power of Christ. It is a quality that inheres in the soul in a permanent and indelible manner making it apt for its function in the Mystical Body.

The Christian ought to exercise this social function in the state of grace and in friendship with God, but by the merciful forethought of the Saviour he can still exercise his power even though he is not in the state of grace. What the Christian owes to others is not his own personal share in the life of grace, but the very fullness of the life of Christ: *Et de plenitudine ejus omnes nos accepimus* [22].

---

[22] John, I, 16.

CHAPTER II

THE SACRAMENTS AS ACTS OF CHRIST

How DO THE sacraments produce grace? Is there not a lack of proportion between the material constituents of a sacrament and the effect produced? Even on the metaphysical plane, not to speak of the transcendent mystery of supernatural life, how can we attribute to matter the power of spiritual action?

In the early ages of the Church these were weighty problems and the Platonic philosophy of the times was unable to provide a fully satisfactory solution. The Fathers met the problem by saying that matter acts on matter and the Spirit of God acts on the spirit of man[1]. They would scarcely have dared to assert that matter acts on the spirit or that the body acts on the soul.

To-day, however, the problem is not so complicated. We have travelled a good distance from the conception of the relations between body and soul as the relations between two complete substances. We accept the fact that the body does act on the soul; this is evident in every act of sensation, sense-perception, and emotion. But when one wishes to apply to the sacraments this law of the exercise of causality by matter on spirit the earlier objections are sustained with apparently greater force than ever.

Granted that the body acts on the soul, it is equally true that the spirit can be affected only by what is also spiritual. If we can say that the body acts on the soul, it must be understood that this is possible only through a reaction of the soul itself, by which the soul actively conforms itself to the data of sense perception and assimilates (on the plane of either sense or intellectual perception) the data supplied by the bodily senses. We conceive abstract ideas, for example, by an active conformity of the intellect with the data offered by the senses.

The sacraments, however, act *"ex opere operato"*—to use the

---

[1] Cf. Cyril of Alexandria: *In Joannem Comment.*, II, 1; III, 5; *P.G.* LXXV. 244.

theological expression—and by this we mean that they ought to produce grace of themselves and not merely by virtue of the reactions of the person receiving them. The recipient must indeed fulfil certain conditions if he is to receive grace, but these conditions do not constitute an exercise of causality in the strict sense of the word. They remain conditions, necessary conditions, for the exercise of sacramental causality.

To maintain that the effect of the sacraments is caused by the personal reactions of the recipient would be to fall into line with Protestantism in its interpretation of the efficacy of the sacraments.

There have been various explanations of the way in which matter can be said to produce a spiritual effect. St. Thomas solves the problem by his theory of instrumental causality. The effect produced by an instrumental cause resembles not the cause itself but the idea in the mind of the principal agent. A bed made by a carpenter does not resemble the tools he used but the plan or idea which he had in mind. The sacraments come into the category of instrumental causes. It suffices, then, that they produce in man what God, the principal agent, has determined that they should produce according to His plan of sanctification[2].

This explanation brought a measure of tranquillity to troubled minds. But on the strictly dogmatic plane there remained the difficulty of admitting that a creature could exercise real causality in producing an effect that was supernatural and divine. Here there is infinite disproportion between the effect and the cause. How can this infinite gap be bridged?

One solution would be to understand the sacraments as the "occasional" causes of grace: the proper fulfilment of the sacramental rites provides the "occasion" for God to infuse grace into the soul. Once the sacramental sign has been completed, God infuses grace, just as a trader hands over merchandise on the receipt of the requisite number of banknotes. By convention, a certain equivalence has been established and accepted between such token money and the real value of the goods delivered. Similarly, God has determined that the infusion of grace through the sacraments should correspond to their valid administration and the fulfilment of certain conditions in the soul of the recipient.

This was the position adopted by the Franciscan school of

---

[2] *S. Th.*, III, Q. 62, a. I, c.

theology, and St. Bonaventure uses scriptural examples to illustrate this occasional causality. In the case of Naaman the leper, for instance, neither the waters of Jordan nor the words of Eliseus had in themselves the power to cure him; but both were the indispensable conditions for his cure.

Likewise the sacraments have not in themselves the power to cause grace, but their reception is necessary because God has made this the condition of His bestowing grace[3].

Duns Scotus elaborated the technical vocabulary of this theory. The reception of a sacrament, he says, constitutes a disposition which calls forth the effect of the sacrament, not by virtue of anything intrinsic in the sacrament capable of producing this effect, nor by virtue of the personal dispositions of the recipient, but by the helping power of God Who alone causes this effect. . . . God has thus arranged things and has revealed to His Church the Divine plan to bestow grace on whoever would receive the sacrament[4].

This theory won a measure of acceptance until the Council of Trent. But when the ancient dictum "the sacraments *contain* grace"[5] was canonised by the Council, the theory of occasional causality was found to be ill in conformity with the supreme Magisterium of the Church and it yielded place to the theory of moral causality. Was this latter explanation an improvement on the former?

In the theology of Melchior Cano[6] and of Vasquez[7], the theory of moral causality did present the elements of a real causality that acted on the principal agent, God, influencing Him to produce the effect of the sacrament. Such influence was in the nature of a prayer that is infallibly granted. In this view, the sacramental rite, by recalling the merits of Christ, is necessarily efficacious before God and results in the bestowal of grace[8].

---

[3] *In IV Sent.*, Dist. I, Pars I, art. 1, q.3.

[4] " Susceptio sacramenti est dispositio necessitans ad effectum signatum per sacramentum, non quidem per aliquam formam intrinsecam, per quam necessario causaret terminum, vel aliquam dispositionem praeviam, sed tantum per assistentiam Dei causantis illum effectum, non necessario absolute, sed necessitate respiciente potentiam ordinatam; disposuit enim universaliter et de hoc Ecclesiam certificavit, quod suscipienti tale sacramentum ipse conferret effectum signatum." (*In IV Sent.. Dist. I, art.* 4).

[5] The expression comes from Hugo of St. Victor.

[6] *Relect. de Sacramentis,* P. VI.

[7] *Disput.* 132, Cap. 5; *Disput.* 133, Cap. 1 and 2.

[8] " Dicimus Christi humanitatem mediis suis meritis fuisse causam miraculorum et Apostolos media invocatione et oratione fuisse instrumenta Dei ad sanitates et

Later Cardinal Franzelin was to say quite simply, "A sacrament is morally an act of Christ"[9]. It may, however, be asked if such a sacrament can be said to *contain* grace? Even if one accepts the more precise elaboration of this theory proposed by Cardinal Billot[10], who describes a sacrament as an objective sign of a divine decree to bestow grace in virtue of the merits of Christ, it is difficult to see how by such intentional causality a sacrament may be said to contain grace.

Fundamentally, the supporters of the theories of occasional and moral causality presuppose, more or less, that God could not sanctify man in and through matter. Let it be noted that in their view Christ is not the physical cause of grace. He is the principal moral cause and the sacraments are secondary moral causes. God alone is the physical cause of supernatural gifts.

One cannot but feel somewhat dissatisfied with this approach, and there is an impression that such causality is more fictitious than real since it is based on a system of conventions. It resembles an agreement between a doctor and his patients that he will be at their service and will give them the remedies they need every time they ring the bell of his clinic. On being restored to health, a patient might say with truth that he was cured by ringing the doctor's doorbell! He could hardly compare this action with the curative value of the remedies administered by the doctor.

The comparison is apt, because Catholic tradition has always laid stress on this aspect of sacramental causality, namely, that the sacraments are remedies with which the Saviour heals all our spiritual infirmities.

There is another current of thought which found patronage early in the history of sacramental theology. It was elaborated by theologians who did not accept as a principle or admit as proven that a sensible sign was in itself incapable of producing a supernatural and divine effect. They argued from the fact of the Incarnation in which matter was brought into intimate union with the

---

alia hujusmodi facienda nempe per modum impetrationis. Apostoli et humanitas Christi meritorie impetrabant a Deo miracula et virtutes quas operabantur. . . . Eadem igitur ratione et minister sacramenti et sacramentum ipsum per quod impetrat dicitur habere potestatem gratiam producendi et eam in se continere." (*Disput.* 132, Cap. 5).

[9] *De sacramentis in gen.*, Th. X.

[10] *De Ecclesiae Sacramentis*, t. I, p. 95 et seq., p. 106 et seq.

Divine Word and acquired a sovereign efficacy in the dispensation of grace.

Viewed in the light of this elevation of matter in the hypostatic union, the sacraments were regarded as an extension and prolongation of the ineffable union between the Word and created matter. God assumed matter into union with Himself, but He did not thereby make Himself a prisoner nor was the divine action shackled and confined by being exercised in a material body.

On the contrary, the Incarnation reveals God acting in and through matter and elevating the material substance so that it plays a rôle in the sanctification of the world. This is the key to the problem of the efficacy of the sacraments.

The development of this explanation of sacramental causality proceeded by two stages. Let us recall that the authors of the theory of dispositive causality were preoccupied with the problem of explaining what effect, if any, was produced by a sacrament that was impeded from causing grace (the effect of a *sacramentum validum sed informe*). They concluded that such a sacrament produced an *ornatus animae,* an embellishment of the soul, which included in itself a claim to the subsequent reception of grace once the obstacle was removed.

It is interesting to note that it was the Franciscan Alexander of Hales who first proposed this theory which was destined to lead to the later theory of the physical causality of the sacraments[11]. The progression is thus described by St. Thomas:

"According to this theory, the sacraments are in some way the efficient cause of the character and the *ornatus animae,* but in regard to grace, they excercise merely dipositive causality"[12]

Did St. Thomas himself hold this two-headed theory of sacramental causality? Or had he already, as some authors maintain, sketched the theory of physical causality[13]?

---

[11] *S. Th.*, IV, q. V, membr 4.

[12] "Respectu ergo primi effectus sunt sacramenta causae aliquo modo efficientes, sed respectu secundi sunt causae disponentes tali dispositione quae est necessitas, nisi sit impedimentum ex parte recipientis." (*In IV*, disp. I, q. 1, a. 4).

[13] Cf. Pars III, q. 62, a. 1. "Causa instrumentalis non agit per virtutem suae formae, sed solum per motivum quo movetur a principali agente. . . . Et hoc modo, sacramenta novae legis gratiam causant; adhibentur enim ex divina ordinatione hominibus ad gratiam in iis causandam." Capreolus does not admit that there was any development in the thought of the Angelic Doctor on this subject, nor does Cardinal Billot. Pourrat, on the contrary (Op. cit., p. 157, note 1) sees in the text quoted a clear allusion to physical causality.

Whatever the answer be, it is certain that after the Council of Trent and to counterbalance the theory of moral causality championed by Vasquez, the advantages inherent in the theory of physical causality were proposed by Cajetan, and later by Suarez.

Whether one admit, in the first instance, that God communicates a supernatural impulse to the sacrament, or say with Suarez that God elicits from the obediential power of matter that which constitutes it as an instrumental cause of grace, the sacraments are in both cases accepted as physical instruments in the production of grace. They are proximate and immediate, though instrumental, causes of grace[14].

According to this school of thought, the sacraments are indeed acts of Christ, since by virtue of their mysterious union with Him they prolong His saving action in the world. The creative and redemptive power of Christ takes possession of the sacramental sign, bestows on it an efficacy that it does not possess of itself, and makes it a real instrument of grace. A sacrament is no longer the bell which summons the doctor; it is the remedy itself with which the doctor cures the patient.

If one attempts to evaluate these different theories of sacramental causality, one must, we believe, deduce from the writings of the Fathers that the theories of physical and moral causality are equally tenable. With the text of St. John before their eyes—"Unless a man be born again of water and the Holy Ghost" (Jn. III, 5) the Fathers affirmed the necessity of the sensible sign for the infusion of the grace of regeneration.

From that point on they diverge. Some maintained that the material element, e.g., the baptismal water, receives a divine energy from the Holy Ghost by which it is endowed with sanctifying power. To quote St. Basil: "If there is any power in the water, it does not come from the water itself but from the presence of the Spirit"[15].

Others seem to insist on the concomitance of two actions—that of the material element and that of the Holy Ghost—thereby seeming to imply occasional causality. As St. Cyril of Jerusalem

---

[14] " Dicendum est non esse impossibile neque implicare contradictionem ut sacramenta sint propria ac physica instrumenta ad gratiam efficiendam, attingendo immediate ac proxime ipsam gratiae productionem." (*In III*, q. 62, a. 4; disp. 9, sect. 1).

[15] *De Spiritu Sancto*, XV, 35; *P.G.*, XXXIV, 131. We find these words quoted *ad litteram* in St. Ambrose, *De Spiritu Sancto*, I, 6, 77; *P.L.*, XVI, 723.

says: "The water is poured from without and the Holy Spirit purifies the soul interiorly"[16]. Cyril of Alexandria puts it that "the spirit of man is sanctified by the Spirit of God, and the body by the sacramental water"[17].

It was normal that in the mediaeval schools that remained faithful to a Platonic view of the universe the trend should have been in favour of occasional causality, which by reaction led to the theory of moral causality. Occasionalism was characteristic of the Franciscan tradition. On the other hand, the current of thought of which St. Thomas became the most authoritative spokesman, tended first to favour dispositive causality and—as a later development—physical causality.

In choosing between these two major solutions to the problem of sacramental causality, we must be guided by what we know of the divinely organised economy of salvation. We are convinced that by studying the divine plan of salvation we shall reach a greater degree of precision in our concept of sacramental causality. This shall be our next concern.

Throughout the work of Redemption there operates a law which is verified in all domains; we may call it the law of salvation through contact. Contact of the Word of God with the sinful world through the Incarnation in which the Humanity of Christ hypostatically united with the Eternal Son, became the meeting point where our universe was brought under the influence of the redemptive Omnipotence of God. Whatever is touched by the sacred Humanity of Christ is touched by the Divine Person of the Saviour acting in that humanity with divine efficacy.

If the world is to be saved by contact with Christ, it follows that this contact must be possible everywhere and at all times as long as there exists a universe to be saved. There is no need that the presence and action of the Incarnate Word abide among us, extending to all points of the compass and reaching men of all generations.

It was for this purpose that Christ founded a visible Church, uniting it to Himself as His Mystical Body. This Body is not united to Him hypostatically, as is His human Body, but it is

---

[16] " Aqua exterius circumfunditur, Spiritus et interius animam abluit absque defectu." (*Catecheses*, XVII, 14; *P.G.* XXXV, 985).

[17] " Spiritu enim sanctificatur hominis spiritus, aqua vero sanctificata corpus." (*In Joannem Comment.*, II, 1 (III, 5); *P.G.*, LXXV, 244).

really and truly His; the bonds uniting it to Him are not mere juridical relations; they are real and ontological with all the reality that is sanctifying grace. For grace *is* an existing reality; it communicates a real life and a real power of action.

Through His Mystical Body Christ remains in contact with the world so that we may—and, indeed, must—say that where the Church is, there also are the presence and the redemptive action of Christ.

It is outside the scope of our study to prove the fact of this mystical identification between the Church and Christ; the principles are stated at length in the Encyclical *"Mystici Corporis Christi"*. We shall content ourselves with applying the theology of the Mystical Body to the sacramental system.

The major conclusion we draw from the mystical identity of the Church with Christ is that the Church is the principle of contact between the Incarnate Word and the men of all ages. She establishes contact between God and man in her ritual actions which are the actions of Christ in and through His Body. Just as the electric current passes along a wire circuit and on reaching a bulb floods it with light, so in each one of the sacraments Christ reaches out to man, saving him with divine grace.

From this definition of the sacraments as organs of contact between Christ and the world we can derive a better idea of the mode of sacramental causality. Unlike His physical Body, which is hypostatically united to the Word, a sacrament is not an *instrumentum conjunctum*. Nevertheless, a sacrament is not something extrinsic to Christ. As an act of His Mystical Body, it is intrinsic to Him as is the Church herself.

This manner of understanding sacramental causality emphasizes an element that seems to be more or less ignored in the theory of moral causality—the action of Christ in and through the sacramental sign. On the other hand, this interpretation eliminates anything like a too arbitrary understanding of physical causality. There is no longer any question of eliciting from the sensible sign, that is, from the obediential power of matter, a supernatural energy which it does not possess.

Still less are we to imagine grace as contained in the sacramental sign like a draught of medicine diluted in a glass of water. Rather this view of sacramental causality respects the rôle which matter has to play in the scheme of redemption.   Matter is a bond between human beings, the meeting place of their activities.   It does not merely form a link between material bodies; it is the condition for union between souls.   For it is by sense-perceptible signs that our souls communicate with each other and engage in the activities of mutual knowledge and love.   Likewise, it is by the sacramental sign that God establishes contact with sinful man and by His grace transforms man into His own image.

Within the scope of our present study, this approach to sacramental causality enables us to see in every sacramental rite an act of Christ, and in and through this act of Christ an act of the Blessed Trinity.   For every act of Christ connotes in some way the action of the whole Trinity.

As we have seen, the Redemption is a work not only of Christ but of the Three Divine Persons, in which each Person acts according to the exclusive characteristic of His own Personality.   The Son became incarnate so that in and through Him the Father might generate sons to the Divine Life; the Holy Ghost, sent by the Father and the Son, brings all those who are born in the Son to their final perfection in the unity and sanctity of Divine Love.

The Son alone became Man.   He alone suffered and died and rose from the dead.   His purpose in doing this was that corresponding to each experience which He shares with us the Father and the Holy Ghost should come and dwell in us more abundantly : *et apud eum veniemus*[18].

What Christ said about the revelation He brought on earth may also be applied to His action among us : to see Christ is to see the Father and to receive from its immediate source the Spirit of the Father and of the Son.   All the words and actions of Christ were a revelation of the Trinity.   He did not say, "He that seeth Me seeth the Divine Nature or the Godhead that is common to the Father and Me."   He said quite explicitly, "He that sees me sees the Father".

In all His acts Christ gives the Blessed Trinity to souls.   His mission as Saviour consists in this communication of life, the Divine Life which He Himself eternally receives from the Father and which with the Father He communicates to the Holy Ghost.   Every act of Christ, then, is charged with all the love of the Father

---

[18] John, XIV, 23.

for the Son, all the love of the Son for the Father. This means that every act of Christ is full of the Holy Ghost, Who is the mutual love of the Father and the Son.

By revealing Himself, Christ also reveals the Father and the Holy Ghost acting in Him. In giving Himself to the world, Christ gives the Father and the Holy Ghost. This is true not only of the mortal life of Jesus, during which He initiates His work as Redeemer, but it is equally true of His abiding and invisible Life in His Mystical Body, in which He continues His redemptive action in the world. Surely it was in this sense that He said: "It is good for you that I go"[19]. He did not mean that it was good that we should be left orphans—*non vos relinquam orphanos*[20]— but that by His coming to live interiorly in us as members of His Mystical Body we should receive a new outpouring of the Father and the Holy Ghost.

Through the presence and activity of the Incarnate Word in the Church, the Blessed Trinity enters into contact with our universe. Christ, active in His Mystical Body, is the Divine Instrument of salvation through which the world of mortal men is transformed and glorified by sharing in the glory of His Resurrection. The sacraments are a prolongation of the Life and action of the Saviour, and they in turn give us the Blessed Trinity.

We shall see this in greater detail when we deal with the sacraments individually. For the moment, let us savour this truth as a general principle. When Christ acts, the whole Trinity is operative.

Commenting on the words of St. Paul, *"All ye who are baptized in Christ have put on Christ"*, St. Basil says that the mention of Christ is equivalent to a mention of the Trinity and connotes "the Father Who anoints, the Son Who is Anointed, and the Holy Spirit Who is the unction . . . for as we believe in the Father and in the Son and in the Holy Ghost, so also we are baptized in the Name of the Father and of the Son and of the Holy Ghost"[21].

The Three Divine Persons are inseparable in their activity, but they are also distinct as Persons within the absolute unity of the

---

[19] ibid., XVI, 7.
[20] ibid., XIV, 18.
[21] " Nam Christi appellatio totius est professio; declarat siquidem et Deum qui unxit, et Filium qui unctus est, et Spiritum qui est unctio. . . . Sicut enim credimus in patrem et Filium et Spiritum Sanctum, sic baptizamur in nomine Patris et Filii et Spiritus Sancti." (*De Spiritu Sancto*, XII, 28; *P.G.*, XXXIV, 116).

Divine Nature. All Three reveal and give themselves where one Person reveals and gives Himself.

Since it is the Son Who is the First-born of every creature, and since He has been entrusted with the mission of revealing God and saving the world, it is in the action of the Son that we receive the Father and the Holy Ghost. The sacraments are the acts of the Son in His Mystical Body; they bring us the Life of the Blessed Trinity, Father, Son and Holy Ghost.

God alone can give us Divine Life; and God is the Blessed Trinity, Father, Son and Holy Ghost. But in the sublime gift of their Divine Life to us the Three Persons have willed to employ the contact of lowly material things—bread and water and wine and oil.

CHAPTER III

BAPTISM

IT WILL HELP us to appreciate the profound significance of this sacrament if we remember that the original manner of conferring Baptism was by immersion. In the rich symbolism of this ancient rite we can best understand St. Paul's teaching on the twofold aspect of Baptism as a sacrament of death and of life: *Mortui estis et vita vestra abscondita est cum Christo in Deo*[1].

The descent into the baptismal waters was a figure of death, of a radical break with the life of sin. His emergence afterwards from the water symbolized the Christian's coming forth into a new life, a true participation in the life of God.

At Baptism the Christian is conformed to Christ in His Death and His Resurrection. What in Christ was death to mortal life and suffering becomes in us death to sin from which we were redeemed by the sufferings of Christ; what in Christ was a resurrection to life in the glorified state becomes in us a birth to the new life of sanctifying grace. Our rebirth and transformation by grace effects in us a veritable resurrection and so unites us with the risen Christ that we pass from the death of sin into newness of life.

It was in this sense that St. Paul could say to the Colossians : "If you are risen with Christ—*Si consurrexistis cum Christo*"[2]. By making us participate in the glorified Life of the risen Christ, grace is the first seed of our own resurrection.

In this assimilation of the Christian to the dying and the risen Christ we must not lose sight of what is its most fundamental aspect. It is an assimilation of persons, a conformity between two persons, between the Eternal Son and the adopted son of God.

Man's divinization by grace is more than a sanctification and elevation of man's nature. It is a transformation and divinization of the whole person whose whole life must henceforth be brought

---

[1] *Coloss.*, III, 3.
[2] ibid., V. 1.

into conformity with the rhythm of Life between the Three Persons in the Blessed Trinity.

Baptism and the other sacraments, each according to its special function, not only confer on and develop in us a created participation in the nature of God, but also a participation in the processions of the Divine Persons within the Trinity.

In the chapter entitled *The Mystery of the Church and the Sacraments,* Scheebens draws a radical distinction (too radical, we think) between what he calls the "medicinal sacraments" (Penance and Extreme Unction) and those which he describes as "sacraments of consecration", because the latter elevate man to a plane that surpasses what is natural for him[4].

It is quite right to distinguish between these two aspects of sacramental life; but can we not say that both are realised in every sacrament? In each of the seven sacraments there is an element of healing and of consecration.

The Blessed Eucharist, for example, while effecting an ineffable union between our souls and Jesus Christ, is also a remedy for our weakness and the sustaining Food of the Christian during his weary pilgrimage here below.

On the other hand, Penance really consecrates the Christian to a renewal of supernatural life, and by a work of reparation and reconciliation that transcends all the powers of human nature it elevates the whole of man's existence to intimate union with God. All the sacraments are both healing and consecrating, for they are all instruments by which the sinner is adapted to the redemptive Life of the Incarnate Word.

In every sacrament there is an indissoluble union between the two functions of reparation and elevation. By conferring grace, they all, in their respective ways, elevate man, since it is the proper function of grace to bring the whole man into a union of perfect harmony with the Person of the Son of God.

Baptism begins this process of harmony and adaptation. It raises man to the divine plane, reproducing in him by grace the genera-

---

[3] *Mysterien des Christentums* published in 1865; re-edited in *Gesammelte Schriften*, Freiburg im Breisgau, 1941. Dom Augustin Kerkvoorde, O.S.B., has published a French annotated translation in the Collection *Unam Sanctam*, t. XV, entitled, *Le Mystère de l'Église et de ses sacrements*, Paris, 1946.

[4] *Op. cit.*, t. II, p. 471 et seqq.

tion of the Son which takes place eternally in God. The eternal generation of the Son is the root cause of Christ's Resurrection, because the humanity of Christ, in virtue of its hypostatic union with the Eternal Son, has a claim to immortality. It is the Divine Person of the Word Who communicates to the humanity of the dead Christ that incorruptibility which is His in virtue of His eternal generation.

From this point of view—and here we are guided by faith—the Death of Christ is a greater mystery than His Resurrection. His Resurrection is understandable as the effect of the Hypostatic Union; His Death presupposes that the human Body of Christ was temporarily withdrawn from the vitalising action of Him Who is Eternal Life, eternally begotten in the bosom of the Father.

The eternal generation of the Son is the cause of the Resurrection of Christ; it is also the cause of the resurrection of man redeemed by Christ, who through grace is brought into close conformity with the mystery of the Eternal Son.

By our birth to grace we are conformed to the eternal generation of the Son, and by grace we are made partakers in the attributes of Him Who is eternally born of the Father. What are these personal attributes?

The first attribute of the eternal generation is that it constitutes a mystery of eternal newness in the bosom of eternal identity. Sharing the identity of the Godhead, the Son has, in an infinite way, that originality and uniqueness and freshness which is characteristic of a person. In the ineffable mystery of His Divine Personality, the Son possesses divinely what even humans share on their lowly level—the uniqueness of incommunicability. His Personality is His alone, unshared with the Father and the Holy Ghost, a secret in which no other can have part.

It is this uniqueness which constitutes the abiding mystery and the profound attractiveness of personality. A person is different from all other persons. Even in the possession of what is common to others, each person possesses it in his own way. On the human plane, we all share the same specific nature, but each one possesses that nature in a unique mode.

The recurrent mystery of human birth does not leave the impression of a mere repetition of what has already happened before, something that is already very familiar to us. With the birth of another human being into the ranks of humanity we are always impressed with his "otherness".

No one stooping over the cradle of an infant thinks that this new life is a pleonasm. This child, we are profoundly conscious, constitutes in himself something new in the world of men; he has his own personal contribution to make to human existence. He is indeed a man like other men with all the generic and specific qualities of man.

In him is fulfilled the definition of man as an *animal rationale;* but in him we see humanity presented in a new way, humanity as it has never been seen before on earth. He is Peter, not James or Paul. Even a whole lifetime spent in getting to know him will still leave him unknown and unfathomable; we cannot penetrate the mystery of his uniqueness as a person.

What then shall we say of that Person Whose special attribute is to be eternally born, Whose eternity is eternal birth? In Him the mystery of newness is also eternal. In response to that eternal uniqueness and incommunicability the Father exults externally in the contemplation of the splendour of His Son.

The Son possesses this newness of life as Son within the bosom of the one and identical Divine Nature. For as the whole Godhead is Father in the Father, so the whole nature of God is Son in the Son. In this seeming paradox our faith finds the most precious revelation of the Infinite.

If we knew nothing of the mystery of distinct Persons Who are One God it would be difficult for us to conceive the Infinite except as something lifeless and inert; we could never reach an idea of the "ever changeless, ever new" that is the life of the Blessed Trinity.

But knowing that within the bosom of the Infinite there is an eternal surge of Life which is the generation of the Son, we also know with certainty that in God immutability is identified with eternal newness of life that does not terminate in the generation of the Son but issues in an ineffable love that is also eternal, the Person of the Holy Ghost.

The birth in grace of the adopted Son of God resembles the generation of the Son in that it also is characterized by newness, not only because Baptism marks the beginning of the life of grace in a soul that was previously without grace, but more especially because the gift of grace is in itself a surge of life, a vital spring that renews itself perpetually . . . *in novitate vitae.*

By his Baptism, and provided he is faithful to his baptismal vows, a Christian can never accept stagnation as the condition of his spiritual life. His whole life and all his activity is endowed with a forward urge. Baptism implants in his soul a germ of motion that strains forward to perpetual progress.

The continuity of this forward striving of the soul is guaranteed by the fact that its life comes from God and in it there is found a participation in the mystery of a Nature that remains eternally the same while eternally surging into newness of life.

This, then, is the mystery of grace which makes us partakers in the Divine Nature—*consortes divinae naturae*—and brings us into a personal relationship with the Three Divine Persons. Born to the life of grace, a Christian is a person generated by the Father in the image of His Only begotten Son.

Furthermore, just as in the Trinity the Divine processions are characterized by the two complementary aspects of immutability and newness, so too in the Christian soul there is the abiding identity of the supernatural gift of grace and the newness and originality of expression which each Christian gives to the life of grace.

As in the Word, the whole Divine Nature is the Son eternally begotten in the bosom of the Father, so in the adopted son of God his supernatural generation is identified with grace itself, that permanent supernatural quality which as the Council of Trent says, "inheres in the soul" [5].

By Baptism, then, Christians enter upon a life that knows no aging, a life that each one lives in a way completely personal to him, each "according to the measure of the giving of Christ"[2]. They become "new men" of whom the Church never ceases to sing: *Isti sunt agni novelli.*

This newness of life through grace is primarily rooted in the depths of the personal being of the newly born Christian. For grace is above all else a new mode of being. But grace does more than transform our mode of being; it also gives us a new mode of acting.

First of all, grace changes our way of looking at things. By his

---

[5] *Sess. VI,* can. 11; Denz. 821.

supernatural birth in the image of the eternal generation of the Word, the Christian receives a new light, the light of faith: *repleti sunt claritate.* The adopted son of God should see all things as the Eternal Son sees them, in the light of the Word of God.

In our preaching perhaps we do not lay sufficient emphasis on this new capacity for seeing divinely which we receive at Baptism and which is the virtue of faith. Undoubtedly the light of faith is not the same as the Beatific Vision, but it prepares the way for it and it is a disposition of the soul enabling it to see and evaluate all things according to God's way of seeing them.

What Tradition calls the act of divine faith consists in judging all reality in a manner that confirms to the Divine Vision of reality. This act presupposes a higher principle of vision, a faculty granted from on high, without which man could never attain to that interior vision that surpasses our human and earthly sense of values.

That higher principle is the infused gift of faith. It inspires acts of faith and by repeatedly making such acts the Christian acquires a stable and constant disposition by which he judges everything according to the Divine point of view. Just as we speak of a man having a correct human outlook when he has the power of looking at things in their objective reality and forming correct judgments about them, so we can say that at Baptism man receives the Divine outlook.

A Christian sees things divinely because he possesses the power of placing himself at the divine viewpoint in relation to everything that forms part of his experience. Divine faith is the dawning in him of a light that is destined to increase with the years and finally burst forth into the full light of glory. It is a light that grows from strength to strength; an illumination that becomes more intense with use. Nothing can equal the freshness and vitality of a mind that plunges its gaze in the eternal light of God.

Grace also adapts the Christian for a new kind of love. *Caritas Dei diffusa est in cordibus nostris*[6]. The infusion of charity into the soul of a baptized person mirrors the eternal love of the Father for the Son, of the Son for the Father, that Love which is the Person of the Holy Ghost in Whom alone all perfection in Heaven and on earth is fulfilled.

---

[6] *Rom.* V, 5.

He is the Spirit of Love in Whom alone we can reach that union with God to which we are called. He is also the Spirit of Truth without Whom we cannot attain to a vital knowledge of the Truth that makes us free.

His love has the same infinite sweep as His Divine Nature, embracing all reality and breathing harmony into our universe, bringing its multiple and contrasting complexity into harmony with the simplicity of God.

In the depth of our souls the love of the Holy Ghost is plenitude of Life soaring back to its divine origin. Without this love sanctity is beyond us and salvation itself is impossible.

In addition to faith and divine charity, the soul of a baptized person also receives the immortal strength of hope which brings with it yet another form of supernatural action. It would be false indeed to limit the exercise of hope to the repetition of those formulae which the Church teaches us to recite along with the acts of faith and charity.

The virtue of hope, like those of faith and charity, is a power in our lives, enabling us to tackle the problem of existence in a new way and helping us to realize the divine programme in our daily Christian life. The adopted son of God must live by faith and charity; but he cannot do this, he cannot perform the slightest supernatural good, he cannot even begin the slightest action in the supernatural order, unless he relies at every step on the strength of God.

This is where the virtue of hope is necessary. It makes the child of God base his whole existence and pivot all his energies on the omnipotence of God. By the virtue of hope we no longer rely on ourselves but on the inexhaustible power of God which He in His mercy places at our disposal. To live as God's child one must believe and love; one must also lean on God's strength.

On the natural plane of merely human action man relies on the support of a material element. If he is not in immediate contact with the ground, he relies on the support of an aeroplane or a ship to enable him to act in the air or on the ocean. The same truth is evident in his moral and social life. Man must be able to count on the support of his milieu if he is to attain moral well-being and social development.

From childhood to death, during his intellectual, moral and

scientific training, and in his professional life, man always relies on the support of the society in which he lives. Without the continual assistance which we expect and receive from organised society existence would be impossible. To perform even the most necessary actions of ordinary existence we must rely on others. Reliance, trust, hope—whatever be the name we give it—is the stabilizing element in life.

There is indeed a deep meaning in the well-known saying "While there is life there is hope"; though we might say with greater truth, "While there is hope there is life". This merely natural hope is but a pale image of the Christian virtue. Since our Christian life is Divine Life, our reliance must be on God alone.

Having received Divine Life as a gratuitous gift of God, the Christian must look to God for all that will help him to live that Life. His supernatural life impregnates all that he is and all that he does, supernaturalizing his whole person in such a way that for him the origin, centre and term of his destiny and that of the whole universe is precisely the development of the Divine Life of grace.

As a result, the life of the adopted son of God should be characterized by that permanent state of hope which we call abandonment. By it he relies solely and uniquely on God.

From all this we can appreciate that faith, hope and charity constitute in the Christian soul new powers of action; just as grace itself is a new mode of being. This divine faith and love and hope and grace itself exist in the Christian soul only when it is conformed to the Eternal Son of God by a supernatural birth that reflects the eternal generation of the Word.

Eternal generation—eternal newness of life; we must also add eternal resemblance. The Son reproduces in Himself the traits of the Father. He is the "figure of His substance—*figura substantiae ejus*".[1] He resembles the Father not only because, like the Father, He, too, is God, but also because He is God born of God, because He is the Son.

We are well aware that a son bears the stamp of his origin in a manner that is completely personal to him. He is a man like other men; but he is also the son of a certain father. Not only does

---

[1] *Hebrews*, I, 3.

he inherit some physical characteristic, but in his character, too, he bears the parental imprint.

Every communication of life by generation entails the mystery of resemblance. In the Blessed Trinity, the Son bears a perfect resemblance to the Father. By virtue of His ineffable generation in the bosom of the Father, He receives a resemblance to the Father which is not shared with the Holy Ghost, even though the Holy Ghost is God equally with the Father and the Son.

The resemblance between the Holy Ghost and the other Divine Persons consists in His possessing the same eternally unchanging Nature of God. But the Son is the eternal image of the Father in virtue of the resemblance that is the unique prerogative of every true generation.

The adopted son of God will also bear a resemblance to his heavenly Father. For Baptism is a true generation by grace in the image of the eternal generation of the Only Begotten of the Father. In this context we can recall the words in which St. Paul speaks of Christ as the "first-born of every creature—*primogenitus omnis creaturae*"[8].

Since all creation comes into existence according to the Divine Exemplar of all things, the Word of God, we must with greater truth assert that every generation in grace has as its prototype the generation of the Eternal Son. Every Christian participates by grace in the generation of the Son and with Him shares the privilege of saying, "Abba, Father".

All this should help us to appreciate the special providence which our heavenly Father has for us. If He loves us so much that He cares for the hair of our head, if all our life should develop in loving confidence and abandonment to Him, the reason is that His love for us has caused in us a real resemblance to Himself. The Father sees in us a reflection of His substance, in an infinitely higher degree than any earthly father sees himself mirrored in the traits of his child.

At our supernatural birth in Baptism, God takes responsibility for us, just as a human father accepts parental responsibility for the destiny of his infant son. The failure of the child is in some sense the failure of the father. His paternity has failed; though

---

[8] *Coloss.*, I, 15.

he has succeeded in generating a son, he has failed to bring that
initial process to its crowning perfection.

The loss of a baptized soul is much more grievous in the eyes
of the Eternal Father. In him creation itself is thwarted for it
issues finally in an object of divine detestation; grace, too, is
thwarted because a son who was born into the Divine Family has
failed. It is easy, then, to understand the special providence with
which the Father surrounds His children.

As the living image of His Father, the Son is thereby a witness
to His Father's glory. Being Son, He manifests the substance of
Him Whose image He is. Within the bosom of the Trinity, the
Son from all eternity bears witness to the Father, and in Him from
all eternity the Father is well pleased. By His birth in time and His
coming among us as the revelation of the Father, the Son continues
this eternal testimony.

Those who have been born to eternal life in the Son have a duty
to share in that mission. Every Christian should reveal the God
Whose seal he bears. He will do this by living in a manner worthy
of his divine sonship, revealing the Father in his words and deeds.
Doing this the Christian continues the mission of the Son of God,
reproducing in his own life the words and acts of Christ: *Sicut
misit me vivens Pater et ego mitto vos*[9] .

Christians are prepared for this mission in the vivifying waters
of Baptism. The significance of the baptismal character is a dis-
puted topic among theologians. That it is a spiritual and indelible
mark is admitted by every Christian—this teaching is enshrined in
revelation. But what is its purpose? And secondly, what is its
nature?

There were divided opinions on these two problems as early as
the Middle Ages. We have already had occasion to recall[10] that
Alexander of Hales regarded the character as a quality determining
a special mode of existence, or, to use scholastic terminology, a
habitus whose principal purpose was to dispose the soul for the
reception of grace and whose immediate effect was a certain resemblance between the soul and Christ the Head of the Mystical
Body[11].

St. Thomas, wishing to differentiate more clearly between the

---

[9] *John*, XX, 21.
[10] Page 26.
[11] *S. Th.*, IV, q. VIII, membr. 8.

grace and the character of the sacrament, classified grace as a *habitus,* and attributed the character to the category of *potentia,* that is, a quality which disposes a subject for action. According to this view, the sacramental character seals a Christian for the exercise of a public function in the Church[12].

According to the Angelic Doctor, every sacramental character disposes the soul for the exercise of divine cult. The specific character of Baptism confers the capacity to receive the other sacraments.

But in what way can one say that the baptismal character orientates the soul for the exercise of a public ministry? According to St. Thomas, it merely enables the Christian to receive the other sacraments, but in doing this it shares in the efficacy of those sacraments which actually do confer the power to exercise public ministry.

From this point of view, the baptismal character is the foundation of the whole Christian edifice, an edifice which is raised by the whole ensemble of acts of cult practised by the Christian. But in itself the baptismal character does not designate the Christian for any precise public function.

St. Thomas does tell us that by Baptism man participates in the priesthood of Christ. Is this an adequate explanation? If such a participation is nothing more than a capacity to receive the other sacraments, it is hard to see how the sacramental character disposes the Christian for anything more than his personal progress in the interior life. The character does not seem to fulfil its rôle as an active power conferring an aptitude to exercise public acts of cult.

If, however, Baptism establishes a vital conformity between the Christian and Christ; if for this reason it implies the mission of giving exterior evidence of his inner Christlike qualities; if the character gives the power to engage in this mission, and if it seals the Christian for the apostolate of bearing witness—can it not, then, be said with strict accuracy that the baptismal character does in fact dispose and empower the adopted son of God to exercise a public function?

This public office derives from the resemblance the Christian bears to the Person of the Son of God. As son, the Christian bears an image of his heavenly Father, and by Baptism he is ordained

---

[12] *S. Th.,* III. q. 63, a. 2, c.

once and for all as a witness to God. He is called to make open and public confession of Christ, even at the cost of his life, even unto martyrdom.

Nor does his profession of faith cease with death; according to the common teaching of theologians, the soul of the damned Christian is still a witness, even in the depths of hell. Though he has been finally and irrevocably cut off from the Divine Family, though he has squandered the inheritance received from his Father, he is still eternally sealed with the stamp of resemblance of Christ. He can never disown his divine origin, even when he has committed the supreme treachery of final impenitence.

He who had been called to a loving and voluntary confession of Christ, continues a witness to Christ, even when he has been finally excluded from the Divine love. He bears forever the seal of his divine origin, the seal of the Blessed Trinity. He received it as a mark of divine love; by it he continues to give witness, even in the abode of hatred.

Regarded in this light, the sacramental character corresponds to the traditional description of it as a spiritual seal, a mark imprinted on the soul (*signaculum sphragis*), comparable to the brand with which a shepherd marks his sheep[13]; on the other hand, our interpretation is in essential agreement with that of St. Thomas, who holds that the character confers a certain power of action, and that it designates the Christian for the exercise of a public function; this function we find in the public confession of faith to which the baptised person is obliged.

Newness of life, resemblance to the Father, the mission of bearing witness—these are the prerogatives of the Divine Sonship of the Word, and at Baptism the Christian is made a partaker in them. There is another prerogative whose vital importance must be stressed: the eternal generation is a source of love.

Since He is God, sprung from God, the Word is necessarily the object of the infinite personal love of the Father; and with the same necessity the Word loves the Father, Who engenders Him eternally with a love that is also infinite and personal. This personal and mutual love inherent in the divine generation of the Son by the Father is the principle from which the Holy Ghost proceeds.

---

[13] Cf. St. Augustine, *Contra Epistulam Parmeniani*, II, 13, 29; P.L. XLIII, 71.

In this love, in the Holy Ghost, the Life of the Son within the Blessed Trinity is finally completed; the same Divine Love determines the place occupied by the adopted son of God in the intimate current of life between the Three Divine Persons. Let us consider this a little longer.

We have said that it is impossible for the Father and the Son not to love with a mutual and eternal love. It is likewise impossible that there should not be an equally eternal Spirit of Love proceeding from the mutual love of Father and Son. This Spirit is a Person, unique and distinct as a Person, as the Father and the Son are unique and distinct. He is the adequate subsistent expression of the love of the Father and of the Son.

The whole Godhead, the total infinity of God is Father in the Father; the same undivided divinity is Son in the Son. The Holy Ghost, perfect expression of the mutual surrender of Father and Son is also the infinite God.

Theses considerations are of capital importance in determining the place which Baptism reserves for the adopted son of God in the Life of the Blessed Trinity.

Like the eternal Son, the adopted son of God is the object of the love of the Father, a love that expresses itself in his supernatural generation to the life of grace. In this generation the Father sends His Only Begotten Son, and this divine gift is the origin of our resemblance to and our union with the Word.

Now, just as the eternal generation is the principle of a subsistent eternal Love, the Holy Ghost Who is in the Father and the Son, similarly since the Father bestows Divine Life on us by sending His Son, and since the Father and the Son love us, they are in us the origin of the Holy Ghost.

No one can have the Divine Life unless he be born of the Holy Ghost. For there is only one way in which we can resemble the Son, the author of our Divine Life, and that is by love, by a life lived in the Spirit of Love.

For his part, too, the adopted son of God must also become a principle of love, and this is made possible by the virtue of charity. The state of grace necessarily includes charity, that gift of the Holy Ghost which gives us an infused participation in the Love of God Himself.

But this charity in us should be the principle of an active and personal donation of ourselves through the exercise of acts of charity. In the act of charity are indissolubly united both the soul's acceptance of the Blessed Trinity within it and the soul's offering of all that it has received through grace.

Consequently, this child of God's predilection shares in the fullness of the Divine Life. He can sit at the table of the Father with the Son and in the Spirit of the Divine Family. Futhermore, with the Father and the Son, he can send the Holy Ghost. He can do this uniquely in his capacity as son of God, that is, in union with the Father and the Eternal Son.

From another point of view, we can say that the Father and Son associate the adopted son of God with all the divine projects, and in and through him They send the Holy Ghost. The exercise of Christian activity which we have still to describe is based on the power given to God's adopted children to unite their personal actions with the act of the Father and the Son by which, in union with the Holy Ghost, they ceaselessly renew the divine harmony of creation.

CHAPTER IV

CONFIRMATION

AT THE OUTSET, we must try to arrive at a clear understanding of the meaning and scope of this sacrament of the living. With his habitual clarity, St. Thomas has given us a résumé of the teaching of tradition. He tells us that since corporeal and sense-perceptible things bear a certain resemblance to spiritual realities, they can help us to understand something of the divine life of grace.

In the development of his bodily life, it is evident that man achieves a special degree of perfection by arriving at adult age (*ad aetatem perfactam*) and by acquiring the power to perform acts which testify to his possession of human nature in its full perfection. To be a man in the full sense of the term means much more than being born; it implies growth to full adult stature.

The same is true of our supernatural life. Man must develop spiritually to a certain fullness of growth; he must reach spiritual adulthood. Herein lies the importance of the sacrament of Confirmation [1].

The words of St. Thomas open up vast perspectives permitting us to see something of the exigencies of spiritual adulthood with its obligation of eliciting perfect or "grown-up" actions (*perfectas actiones hominis agere*) and underlining the vital intrinsic connection between Confirmation and Baptism.

What God achieves in the Christian soul is a real life which, like the life of all living things, must develop from infancy to full vig-

---

[1] *S. Th.*, III, q. 72, a. 1, c. " Quia vero sensibilia et corporalia gerunt spiritualium et intelligibilium similitudinem, ex his quae in vita corporali aguntur, percipere possumus quod in spirituali vita gratiae speciale existat. Manifestum est autem quod in vita corporali specialis quaedam perfectio est quod homo ad perfectam aetatem perveniat et perfectas actiones hominis agere possit; unde et Apostolus dicit (1 Cor. 13) *Cum autem factus sum vir evacuavi quae erant parvuli*. Et inde est etiam quod praeter motum generationis, quo aliquis accipit vitam corporalem, est motus augmenti, quo aliquis perducitur ad perfectam aetatem. Sic igitur et vitam spiritualem homo accipit per baptismum, qui est spiritualis regeneratio; in confirmatione autem homo accipit . . . quasi quandam perfectam aetatem spiritualis vitae. . . . Et ideo manifestum est quod confirmatio est speciale sacramentum ".

orous maturity. This life restores its diminished energies by utilizing the means offered by its environment to nourish and increase its strength. It comes to grips with hostile forces and develops as the result of constant effort.

But during the various stages of its development the life of a living being remains one and identical. This, too, is a characteristic of the Christian life; it is always the same Divine Life which grows and develops by assimilating the rich treasures of grace contained in the sacraments.

Confirmation is the sacrament which brings the Christian, born of water and the Holy Ghost, to the perfection of adult age. To penetrate some degree into the mystery of Confirmation, we must examine carefully what characterizes Christian life in its full maturity.

Primarily we must examine what constitutes practical Christianity and how it has been understood since the beginning of the Church. We shall see that St. Thomas has simply adopted the most authentic tradition which regarded Confirmation as the sacrament of Christian maturity.

As was made manifest at the first Pentecost, Confirmation marks the full flowering of the Christian life, and from an early date it was considered as the sacrament in which the Holy Ghost brings Christians to full maturity.

Towards the middle of the third century, St. Cyprian, while explaining the meaning of the imposition of hands on the baptized Christian, also testifies to the practice of the Church at that time.

"The Samaritans," he says, " had received true Baptism and that sacrament could not be administered again. They lacked but one thing, and they received it from Peter and John by prayer and the imposition of hands: the Holy Ghost was given them. This practice is still continued among us. The neophytes are presented to us, and by our prayer and the imposition of hands they receive the Holy Ghost, and are brought to perfection by receiving the divine seal" [2].

---

[2] " Quia legitimum et ecclesiasticum baptisma consecuti fuerant, baptizari eos (Samaritanos) ultra non oportebat, sed tantummodo quod deerat, id a Petro et Joanne factum est, ut oratione pro iis habita et manu imposita invocaretur et infunderetur super eos Spiritus Sanctus (Act., VIII, 14 et seqq.) Quod nunc quoque apud nos geritur, ut qui in ecclesia baptizantur, praepositis ecclesiae offerantur et per nostram orationem ac manus impositionem Spiritum Sanctum consequantur et signaculo dominico consummentur ". (*Epistulae*, LXXIII, 9; *P.L.*, III, 1115).

St. Cyril of Alexandria, after speaking of Baptism and the Blessed Eucharist, says "Next comes the use of oil *(ἡ τοῦ ἐλαίου χρεία)* which perfects those who are baptised in Christ *(συντελοῦσα πρὸ τελείωσιν)*"[3].

The same thought is developed by the author of the *De Sacramentis,* who takes pains to show how the reception of the Holy Ghost influences every domain of Christian life:

"To-day you have heard about the spiritual seal which is received after Baptism. The soul regenerated by water must be brought to perfection, and this is done when, through the invocation of the priest, the Holy Ghost is infused into the soul, the Spirit of wisdom and understanding, the Spirit of counsel and fortitude, of knowledge, of piety, and of the fear of the Lord— in a word, the seven fruits of the Spirit"[4].

We have already seen how St. Thomas understands this "perfection of life". Perfect life is adult life. The next point to consider is what are the characteristics of an adult?

Admittedly, adulthood is characterized by a fullness of mental and physical growth which manifests itself in the handling of life's problems. If, however, we wish to follow the path traced by St. Thomas and seek analogies from the sense-perceptible world to attain a better understanding of spiritual realities, we must say that what especially characterizes adult life is strength: strength that manifests itself in mastery over the resources of life.

It cannot be denied that tradition has always attributed an analogous effect to the sacrament of Confirmation which, in the words of St. Ephraem, invests us with the armour of the Spirit[5]. The Decree for the Armenians states that the Holy Ghost is given to us in Confirmation as He was given to the Apostles at Pentecost, to strengthen us—*ad robur*[6].

This teaching was already enshrined in the *Summa Theologica* where St. Thomas tells us that in the sacrament of Confirmation

---

[3] *In Joelem Comment,* 32; *P.G.,* LXXIII, 373.

[4] " Sequitur (baptismum) spiritale signaculum quod audistis hodie legi; quia post fontem superest ut perfectio fiat, quando ad invocationem sacerdotis Spiritus Sanctus infunditur, spiritus sapientiae et intellectus, spiritus consilii atque virtutis, spiritus cognitionis atque pietatis, spiritus sancti timoris; septem quasi virtutes Spiritus." (*De Sacramentis,* III, 2, 8; *P.L.,* XVI, 434).

[5] *Interpretationes in S. Scripturam,* in Joel., 11, 24; *A.S.,* I, 252.

[6] *Denz.* 697.

the fullness of the Spirit is given us for our spiritual strength—*ad robur spirituale*[7].

There is danger, however, of regarding this strength-giving sacrament in a too restricted sense, in a sense that one cannot help feeling is at variance with the traditional trend of Christian thought. It would be a mistake to think that the strength received in Confirmation is primarily and uniquely strength to enable us to struggle against the enemies of Christ and of the Church.

This combat is indeed an integral part of Christian life, and without doubt the gift of the Holy Ghost which the Christian receives in Confirmation includes the strength he needs to triumph over the enemies of his salvation. But life is more than a struggle whose efforts are directed at what may be called a negative result —the withstanding of external assault.

Life is, first and foremost, an immense constructive effort; the toil and labour it involves is directed towards producing something positive. In the article from the *Summa* from which we have already quoted St. Thomas describes adulthood as that period of life in which man communicates to others what he has achieved by his own personal activity: *cum ad perfectam aetatem pervenerit incipit jam communicare actiones suas ad alios*[8].

The point of view expressed by St. Thomas is a faithful reflex of Christian tradition. Life expresses itself in achievement; it calls for the exercise of all the resources of the living being in view of communicating something to others. An adult is primarily a worker. Only when he begins to work for his daily bread and for the support of his dependents does a man cut himself off most decisively from childhood.

The struggle in which he engages as an adult is not a mere defensive campaign against enemies that threaten his life; it is something much more profound, it is a great positive struggle. In his work, man is pitted against all the forces of resistance inherent in matter, he comes to grips with nature and all her varied resources in a struggle to bring them into obedience to his will.

Confirmation makes us workers. The manner in which the Redemption of the world is to be achieved made it necessary that there should be such a sacrament. The world can find salvation

---

[7] *S. Th.*, III, q. 72, a. 2, c.
[8] ibid.

only in the one Saviour. For this reason it must always and everywhere come under the influence of the redemptive power of Christ.

To make this possible He has willed that the world should be saved by an immense collective effort on the part of all the members of His Mystical Body, working in close and constant collaboration with the supernatural grace which resides in Him in all its plenitude.

In this task, which the Apostle calls "the edification of the Body of Christ", every member of the Church must contribute all that he has and all that he is. The work of the Christian apostolate is not a work of supererogation. It is the perfect expression of the inner vitality of the Church which tends of itself to spread and communicate itself abroad.

Confirmation is the normal complement of Baptism. Its purpose is not simply to help the Christian to live his personal life as a son of God; Baptism already fills that rôle, and a baptised person who dies before receiving Confirmation, provided he has retained sanctifying grace, possesses Divine Life, and he is truly a temple of the Blessed Trinity.

Confirmation adds something to Baptism, completing and perfecting it as the flower perfects the plant, or as that extra quality which we call "genius" adds a further perfection to human intelligence.

Just as human nature contains in itself the potentialities of genius —even though man can live his life without ever reaching that degree of perfection—so, too, man's participation in the Divine Nature by the grace of Baptism is ordained to the fuller development of that life which is effected by the sacrament of Confirmation.

The passage from spiritual infancy to adult Christianity can be seen exemplified in the effect of the first Pentecost on the disciples of Jesus. The coming of the Holy Ghost caused an astonishing transformation that was immediately manifest, both in the intellectual and practical spheres.

The disciples already possessed a knowledge of the prophecies of the Old Testament and of the promises made to Israel; but on the day of Pentecost their minds were flooded with new light which

---

⁹ *Ephes.* IV, 16.

gave them an assured and profound understanding of the inner meaning of the prophetic books. For the first time in their lives, they saw and understood that everything in the history of Israel was part of a vast and meaningful canvas; everything led up to the Death and Resurrection of our Lord.

Mere knowledge of the prophets had not sufficed; they needed the gift of understanding to enable them to grasp the full significance of what the prophets had foretold. Here we have one of the marks of adulthood; an adult has a mature intelligence that grasps the deeper significance of things.

On the plane of action what an astounding transformation was immediately effected! What driving force, what assurance characterizes these erstwhile timid men! Nothing can check their efforts to spread the knowledge of Christ and to build up the spiritual edifice of the Church.

They act with decision; their courage in enduring persecution seems effortless. In a word, they act with strength. The crowds who heard them were impressed by their courage, not so much because they were dauntless in opposing the angry leaders of the Jewish people, but because they were men obviously dedicated to the reconstruction of a new world, a world of the Spirit.

The sudden transformation of the Apostles on Pentecost explains better than anything else how necessary it was that Christ should ascend into Heaven—the *expedit vobis* which they had failed to grasp on Holy Thursday night. His going was the indispensable condition for the outpouring of the Holy Ghost. *Si enim non abiero Paraclitus non veniet ad vos*[11].

In the inspired activity of the first years of Christianity we can get a better understanding of the divine plan of redemption: God builds nothing without the collaboration of human workers. The Church to-day is identical with the Church of the Apostles. At each successive moment of its development, at each stage in its expansion, day by day throughout the life of the Church, Pentecost is renewed. Christians born to Divine Life in Baptism are brought to maturity in the sacrament of Confirmation, which makes them adult workers in the scheme of redemption.

Man cannot play his part as a worker in the plan of redemption

---

[10] John, XVI, 7.
[11] ibid.

unless he is conformed to Christ. The sole purpose of all the sacraments is to effect this conformity between the Christian and his Saviour. With regard to the sacrament of Confirmation, we may enquire, "In what way is Christ a worker?"

The first and obvious answer is that Jesus spent the thirty years of His hidden iife as a humble Artisan. Indeed the fact that God Incarnate showed a preference for this kind of life should create in the human heart a sincere admiration for manual work and should arouse in manual workers a feeling of legitimate pride in the thought of the Saviour devoting Himself to the same kind of tasks, spending Himself in a toilsome occupation that called for the exercise of His full human energies.

But the life of Jesus in Nazareth was a greater mystery than appears at first glance. The manual work done by the Son of God in the carpenter's shop was an external manifestation, we might almost say a parable, of the universal work of redemption which He had already commenced.

By becoming an Artisan, Our Lord was in some sort making public profession of His essential function in the world: He was come among us as the Artisan of Redemption. To this task He devoted all His powers of mind and heart; its execution cost Him every drop of His Precious Blood. In redeeming the world, Christ employed all the resources of His humanity; more than this, He employed all the resources of His divinity and of His Divine Personality.

Every act, every effort, every suffering experience of Jesus Christ was launched and controlled and brought to fruition by the Divine Person of the Word.

Here let us recall the philosophical truth that every human act is the act of the person who performs it (*actiones sunt suppositi*). In Christ the Person Who acted was the Word of God. It follows that when we say that Christ was the Artisan of our Redemption we must understand this not only with reference to His human nature but to His Divine Person.

It was the Divine Personality of the Word which gave infinite value to the least actions of Jesus; the same Divine Person is the source from which grace derives its saving efficacy.

Since the Person of the Word is eternal, and since traditional Catholic thought sees the Word as the archetype of all creation—

omnia per Ipsum facta et sine Ipso factum est nihil[12]—it would seem that the rôle of Worker or Artisan adopted by Jesus in Nazareth and His rôle as the Artisan of our Salvation correspond to a personal attribute of the Son within the bosom of the Blessed Trinity.

The Son of God has been appointed by the Father to perform a work on earth. Did He not frequently refer to this Himself? "My Father worketh until now and I also work"—"*Pater meus usque modo operatur et ego operor*"[13].

It follows from this that if, by the sacrament of Confirmation, the Christian is brought into conformity with Christ the Worker, he is also called to a deep resemblance with the Person of the Son.

Following the law of analogy, we can detect two principal elements in this resemblance: firstly, the confirmed Christian will participate in the universal creative power of the Word; and secondly, he will share the secret of adapting the redemptive love of God to all men in all circumstances, everywhere and until the end of time.

Confirmation confers the power of participating in the universal creativeness of the Word "by whom all things were made"—"*per quem omnia facta sunt*". The Word is the archetype and Divine Model of all created being and perfection that issues from the creative power of the Father; He is, likewise, the Divine Exemplar of every renewal of that creation.

This is the reason why the Redemption, which is essentially a new creation, a renewal of our sin-ravaged world, must be attributed to the Eternal Son with even greater reason than the first creation.

The Christian's participation in the universal rôle of the creative Word entails that he become an apt co-worker in every Christian endeavour and that he play an adult part in the reconstruction of the world and of human society in Christ. Confirmation does not constrict Christian life and effort within the limits of what are officially listed as pious or charitable activities. It affects the whole range of human action in which the son of God engages. His new life of grace must permeate and vitalise every domain of human effort, every walk of life, every profession.

Only by christianizing all the liberal professions, all the manual

---

[12] John, I, 3.
[13] John, V. 17.

arts, only by infusing the Spirit of love and justice into the domains of medicine, law, engineering, commerce and banking, can the Redemption be fully achieved. Only on this condition can the world be "re-established in Christ" and become in truth the *terra nova,* the new earth, resplendent with the light of the Resurrection.

No wonder, then, that Confirmation should be *par excellence* the sacrament of strength. Merely to think of undertaking this superhuman task, much more to bring it to a successful issue, requires courage and endurance and an inexhaustible fund of supernatural dynamism.

Strength and courage are a *sine qua non* because of the truly universal character of the Christian mission and also because the building up of the new Christian world, like the Incarnation itself, is a task that entails a vast re-adaptation of human values and a constant solicitude to bring those values into harmony with the supernatural order.

Our earth, in the throes of perpetual labour, our human society, forever haunted by a restless striving for progress, must open its portals to receive the eternally immutable God. The totality of God and His divine values must conquer, without destroying, the totality of human values.

This means that for its salvation the world at every instant of its evolution and in every cell of its vast organism needs the limitless patience of an apostolic energy that combines the suppleness of the spirit with the tenacity of divine love. Confirmation bestows these divine gifts on the Christian soul.

In the early Church, the gifts of the Holy Ghost were manifested in all their rich fullness. The small band of Jews chosen by the Lord as His apostles had to confront and preach the Gospel to a hostile and uncircumcised generation. Turning their backs on the Synagogue, they faced the barbarian gentile world, offering it the new wine of the Christian promise, and practising with dauntless intrepidity a programme of redemptive conquest that they expressed in the words, "Christ is all in all"[14].

In our own day, the influence of the gifts of the Holy Ghost, though less visible, is none the less constant in every phase of Christian life. The Church needs an ever greater number of adult Christians because she is still far from having attained her full

---

[14] Coloss., III, 11.

stature and because she has to achieve that full development within the framework of a world that is much more ancient than she is.

The need is all the more acute because of the lack of synchronization between the rate of growth in the Church and the rate of development of society on the merely human plane. The rate of human progress is very rapid; the Church is regulated by eternity. How can the one find place in the other? How can the fast-changing aspects of society be reconciled with the changelessness of the Church?

It seems an impossibility. But Catholic action through the centuries has not shirked the challenge, and in our day she grapples with the problem in every domain, in the realms of art and science and in the complexities of economic and political evolution. When man achieves a new degree of progress in any sphere he is tempted to believe that he has outstripped the Church. He may feel that he can do without her altogether.

To be cured of his heady intoxication, man must be brought to a realization of the true meaning of progress, both in his own specialized field and in the life of the Church. He must be brought to the point of admitting that the primary problem is not one of the relative speed of development; it is a problem of equilibrium, a problem of establishing harmony.

To grasp the nature of this problem, and, more especially, to offer a concrete solution, calls for the exercise of adult qualities. Only an adult mind can grasp that there is a complex problem of human equilibrium; only an adult can offer a lasting solution.

The Christian engaged in the heroic task of building up the Body of Christ needs an abundance of heavenly wisdom and prudence; he needs them in a higher degree than is conferred in the sacrament of Baptism. He needs the gifts of the Holy Ghost in such plenitude that even long sustained effort becomes easy. He needs the Holy Ghost within him, consuming his soul with divine fire; he needs the breath of the Spirit to inspire and carry him onwards in his task as collaborator with Christ in the salvation of the world.

All this he receives in the sacrament of Confirmation. For though this sacrament conforms the baptised person to the Person of the Word in His rôle as Creator and Saviour, it is in a special way the sacrament of the Holy Ghost. This for a twofold reason:

firstly, the Spirit of God is the link, the bond of union, between the creature and God. His personal attribute within the Blessed Trinity is that He is the subsistent bond of union between the Father and the Son; in His mission on earth He cements and stabilises the union between the members of the Mystical Body and their Head.

Secondly, Confirmation is as it were a reinforcement of the sacrament of Baptism; it is the sacrament of the plenitude of God's gift to man. As such, as the sacrament of divine plenitude, it is the sacrament of the Holy Ghost, Who within the Trinity closes and completes the cycles of inter-Trinitarian life.

The eternal surge of love that flows from the Father to the Son, and from the Son to the Father, is a plenitude of love that is completed in the procession of the Third Divine Person, the Holy Ghost. Similarly in the works of God *ad extra* (which are common to the Three Divine Persons) wherever God's gifts are characterized by superabundant fullness, we might almost say by divine excess, —*in mensuram plenitudinis*— there we recognize the Holy Ghost.

We cannot come to the Father, we cannot be united to the Son, except through the fullness of the Spirit. He it is Who first introduces us to the Father and the Son in Baptism when we are born into the Divine Family through water and the Holy Ghost. Likewise, in the sacrament of Christian maturity, it is the Holy Ghost Who brings us the Father and the Son in a new and special manner.

Confirmation—to repeat—brings the Christian to full maturity and enables him to exercise adult Christian activity, namely, to collaborate in the building-up of the Mystical Body of Christ. Confirmation does this by conforming the Christian to the Person of the Word in His creative and redemptive rôles. By this very fact, Confirmation also establishes a bond of greater intimacy between the adult Christian and the Eternal Father.

The Almighty Father, Whose Son is His Image, and Who has treated all things through His Word, invests us with a participation in His power. Since Confirmation destines the Christian for the task of building a new world, he needs some share in the power of the Father. As son of God by adoption, he is, like the Eternal Son, a creator of immortal beauty; like the Son, too, he receives from the Father the secret of Divine success; and in his work for the reconstruction of the world, he will further resemble the Son "by whom also He made the world—*per quem fecit et saecula*"[15].

Endowed with a share in the power of the Father, acting as an instrument of the Father, the Christian is equipped to restore all things in the image of the Son. For Christian action in the world consists precisely in bringing Christ into the world and investing both men and things with a new form of existence, a divine glory that transcends all the natural pretensions of the mere creature. Grace is that new reality, a new dimension, as it were, which transforms the whole sweep of human life in its spiritual and material relations.

At the Head of this transformed and grace-filled universe stands the figure of Christ, the absolute norm and the ideal perfection of the new world. And in this new creation the Christian, according to the grace that is in him, radiates the power of the Father, the image of the Son and the plenitude of the Holy Ghost. This plenitude of the Holy Ghost, this superabundant charity, this ocean of divine light is the inexhaustible powerhouse that supplies the energies employed by the Christian in the reconstruction of the world.

It is clear, then, that Confirmation derives its special efficacy from the Three Persons of the Blessed Trinity and that it establishes the soul in a new relation with the Divine Persons. Just as in Baptism the Father, Son and Holy Ghost brought the soul forth to a participation in Their Divine Life, so in Confirmation the Three Divine Persons flood the soul of the adopted son of God with a new and distinct outpouring of grace which makes the Christian participate intimately in the creative and redemptive action of the Blessed Trinity.

To conclude this chapter, we shall now consider the manner in which Confirmation is conferred and we shall probe the symbolism of the sacramental rite as a key to the effects which the sacrament produces. The matter of the sacrament is the anointing of the forehead with holy chrism, accompanied by the imposition of hands— a gesture which perpetuates the action of the Apostles when they called down the Holy Ghost on the first Christians.

What is the symbolism of this anointing with a mixture of chrism and balsam? The Roman Catechism gives us the answer: the oil signifies the plenitude of grace which descends on us from

---

[15] Hebrews., I, 2.

Christ our Head and which the Holy Ghost distributes through the members of the Body. Balsam signifies the sweet odour of the virtues and also symbolizes protection against contagion.

In this explanation we can grasp the fact—so often repeated in the preceding pages—that the fundamental reality in the sacrament of Confirmation is a new plenitude of life.

It is worth noting that the symbolic anointing which the Church uses to indicate the meaning of this sacrament is not explained by the Catechism as an anointing of the Christian athlete for the arena of life; it is rather a symbol of the full development of inner strength and divine vitality which will find expression in the manifold tasks and duties of life, and not least in the practice of the "peaceful" virtues, such as patience, gentleness and humility.

At the same time, by conferring a plenitude of inner strength, Confirmation *does* indeed arm the Christian for combat; for he, like every man of action, must be ready to do battle in defence of his Divine Life.

The efficacy of the rite of Confirmation derives from the fact that the sacrament is conferred in the name and by the power of the Blessed Trinity. The sacramental formula used in the Latin Church explicitly mentions the Trinity as the principal agent responsible for bringing the soul to full Christian maturity: "I sign you with the Sign of the Cross and I confirm you with the chrism of salvation in the Name of the Father and of the Son and of the Holy Ghost".

The same formula is implicit in the words of the Greek rite: "the sign of the gift of the Holy Ghost". For when the Holy Ghost is given, the Father and the Son are also present.

The action of the Blessed Trinity in Confirmation results not only in the bestowal of a fullness of grace; it also imprints a sacramental character. How, we may ask, does the character of Confirmation differ from that of Baptism? If Confirmation enriches Christian life with something analogous to the perfection which maturity adds to natural life, we understand immediately that there is a twofold error to be avoided in speaking of the character of Confirmation.

The first error would be to consider Confirmation in complete isolation from Baptism and to ignore the necessary continuity that exists between them. The second mistake would be to assert a simple and complete identity between the two sacraments.

Only by a sound understanding of the conditions that govern the development of all life, both natural and supernatural, shall we be able to steer a course equidistant from both errors.

In the first place, we must admit without equivocation that the vital principle in a living being remains identically the same through the whole course of life. No one would venture to maintain that at each successive stage in the evolution of vegetable life a new vital principle should intervene to effect the mysterious transformation of the seed into the mature fruit-bearing plant.

The continuity and intrinsic finality that characterize the vital process are sufficient evidence that the same immanent principle of life directs the whole period of growth. Growth in Divine Life is no exception to this law. Here, too, there is a single identical principle of life—sanctifying grace. Gratuitously conferred from on high (*desursum*), grace in the soul is the root of that intrinsic finality which directs all the activity of a Christian in view of the fullest possible development of his Divine Life.

On the other hand, this continuous identity of life manifests itself in an astonishing variety of achievements. Life, one and indivisible in itself, presents many different aspects at the various stages of growth.

The chubby rosy-cheeked infant whimpering in its cradle may one day grow into a stern, well-muscled boxer; but the transformation takes place only as the result of a complex assimilative process that enriches the infant life with powers and qualities so diverse that finally the boxer is scarcely recognisable as the same person.

The same law of growth obtains in the development of the Divine Life of grace. Strictly speaking, growth in Divine Life cannot be called a metamorphosis. (Baptism, however, did effect a metamorphosis when it transformed a man into a child of God). Rather must we say that Divine Life grows by a series of changes so prodigious that the child who was born of water and the Holy Ghost grows up into a Christian adult who is scarcely recognisable as the same person. He is as different from what he was as the Apostles before and after Pentecost, even though he remains the same living being and it is the same life which has now come to its full maturity and strength.

Grace in its mature development presents the phenomenon of an abiding identity that manifests itself in a wide diversity of achievement. It is precisely this diversity in the development of grace that justifies the distinction between the character of Confirmation and that of Baptism.

To repeat: a sacramental character is a spiritual and indelible mark that designates the Christian for the exercise of a public function; a character confers a certain power of action. The power conferred at Baptism, according to the interpretation given in the preceding chapter, designates the new-born Christian to act as a witness to Christ.

The adult Christian, that is, the confirmed Christian, is called to do something more than make a simple profession of faith by the manner in which he lives his daily life; the testimony expected of him is the testimony of apostolic action. He is sealed as an adult Christian worker, pledged to work for the transformation of his milieu and for the construction of the new Christian universe.

Instead of confining his testimony within the limits of his personal life—even though such testimony exercises a real influence by way of example—the adult or confirmed Christian radiates Christ in society and in the organisation of the material world. Even as a man, he is impelled by the inner force of his life to extend his influence beyond the confines of his own personality.

Can one imagine an artist whose creative talent has reached the peak of maturity and who would refuse to create? Can one imagine a successful research scientist who would refuse to bequeath to posterity the fruit of his discoveries?

Just as all life from the moment of birth strives towards the perfection of adulthood, so every adult feels in himself an inner necessity that impels him to prolong his personality in some work of production.

In striving to realise this inner drive, man comes up against many external obstacles, such a strong barrier of resistance, that he needs an energy and a strength that he did not possess in infancy. He needs new strength if his endeavours are to be crowned with success. To sustain him in his efforts towards final victory, he needs the strength of mature manhood.

It is precisely such a strength, the mature strength of Christian adulthood, that the character of Confirmation imprints on the

Christian soul. Confirmation implants in the soul both an impelling need to expend oneself without measure in the service of the Church, and the power to mirror forth in every phase of life the creative power of the Father and of the Son and of the Holy Ghost.

CHAPTER V

PENANCE

It is not a calumny against Christians to say that many of them, even devout souls, regard Penance as a second-rate sacrament. Admittedly, like all the sacraments, Penance is a channel of Divine Life, and this fact alone should suffice to guarantee its prestige as an instrument of divine pardon. But there remains the fact that we who draw upon the spiritual riches of this sacrament are recruited from the inglorious ranks of sinners.

It is something of a humiliating experience to have to confess one's sins to a man in whom we do not always see the minister of Christ. Hence it comes that in the opinion of many people Penance is tinged with the unattractiveness of the sinful consciences with which it deals. Compared with the Blessed Eucharist, which is *par excellence* the sacrament of union with God, compared with Holy Orders and Matrimony and Baptism, Penance seems like a poor relation.

It lacks the dynamism with which Confirmation launches the Christian on his crusade to rebuild the world; it lacks the delicate pathos of Extreme Unction which prepares man to face death.

Among the sacraments, Penance alone seems unattractive. It conjures up the atmosphere of a laundry with its piles of dirty linen, or it suggests the long lines of unfortunates who wait in the corridors of public clinics.

In spite of this, Penance is a new and wondrous revelation of the Heart of God. It is a perpetual fount of forgiveness; it is an abiding testimony to the divine attribute of limitless mercy. Further, Penance comes to us a divine blending of justice and mercy; it is a sacrament of mercy only in so far as it dispenses perfect justice; it dispenses justice by granting divine forgiveness. In it "justice and mercy have kissed".

In this seeming paradox lies all the mystery of the Sinner's Sacrament. We are tempted to see only the humiliating side of it.

Letting our minds dwell on the confession of our secret wretchedness, we are somewhat blind to the mystery that is at work.

There is indeed a paradox in the harmony of justice and love. With our limited vision, we are accustomed to separate the two; sometimes we see them in opposition, as if the triumph of justice entailed the exclusion of love. Or, again, we may be tempted to think that since Christianity is a religion of love, the exercise of justice should gradually be superseded by the exercise of love.

In the following pages we should like to show that the sacrament of Penance solves this paradox; that the constituent elements of the sacrament (the matter and form) find their full meaning only in the close identification between justice and love; that it is precisely in this identification that the sacrament of Penance is an efficacious sign of God's mercy; and, finally, that Penance intimately associates the repentant sinner with the inner life of the Blessed Trinity.

At the beginning it will be well to recall what every Catholic holds as part of the solid tradition of the Church on the subject of Penance.

Our Lord not only promised that He would give the Apostles the power to forgive sin; He actually conferred this power on them after His Resurrection when He said, "Receive ye the Holy Ghost. Whose sins ye shall forgive they are forgiven them, and whose sins you shall retain they are retained"[1].

He placed no restriction on the power He gave them. When He said "whose sins", it is the same as if He had said "all sins" without limitation. The power He bestowed on them was a continuation of His own power as Redeemer, which as He Himself said was universal: *Data est mihi omnis potestas*[2].

By the way they spoke and acted from the beginning of their ministry, the Apostles made it clear that they did not recognize any limitation to their power of forgiving sin. When St. Paul wrote to the Corinthians telling them of his intention to visit them, he said that he was afraid that he might not find them as well disposed as he would wish—*non quales volo*[3].

He feared that they had fallen into such grave sins as sedition,

---

[1] John, XX, 23.
[2] Matthew, XXVIII, 18.
[3] II Cor., XII, 20.

impurity and fornication, and that they were not prepared to repent sincerely. This is equivalent to saying that these sins could be forgiven on condition that they were the object of sincere repentance.

There is a passage in the Apocalypse which also indicates the universality of the power to forgive sin. The Angel of the Church of Thyatira is reprimanded because he allowed Jezabel, a woman who claimed to be a prophetess, to seduce the faithful, leading them to commit fornication and to eat meat that was sacrificed to idols. "And I gave her a time that she might do penance and she will not repent of her fornication"[4].

It is to be noted that the eating of food sacrificed to idols is here equiparated with idolatry and is therefore ranked among the gravest mortal sins.

Since it includes the power "to forgive" and "to retain" sins, it follows that the sacrament of Penance, by the conditions of its divine institution, necessarily includes the power to pass judicial sentence.

How can one decide whether there are grounds for granting pardon or for withholding forgiveness unless one has the power to judge? How can a prudent judgment be passed unless one is aware of the condition of the penitent's soul?

The scope of the divine promise and the words used by Our Lord in conferring the power to forgive sin imply that the granting of pardon is an act of justice and can be done only by judicial procedure.

Later we shall dwell on the grandiose mystery of this close harmony between justice and mercy. For the moment, we simply state the fact that justice and love are indissolubly united in the sacrament of Penance.

The forgiveness of sin presupposes an act of judgment on the part of the confessor; this in turn implies an admission of guilt on the part of the penitent. In other words, the actual confession of sin is an essential element in the sacrament of Penance.

That confession of sin was a practice in the Church at the end of the first century can be seen from a text of the *Didache Apostolorum*: "Thou shalt confess thy sins in church and thou shalt

---

[4] Apoc., II, 18-22.

not engage in prayer with a conscience burdened by sin "[5]. And again: "On Sunday you shall come together to break bread and to give thanks after having confessed your sins "[6]

The same recommendations are contained in the Letter of Barnabas: "Thou shalt confess thy sins and not give thyself to prayer with a sullied conscience "[7].

Origen thus refers to Church practice at the beginning of the third century: "If we make known our crimes not only to God but also to those who have the power to heal our wounds and wash away our stains, our sins will be forgiven by Him Who declared ' I have blotted out thy iniquities like a cloud and thy sins as a mist' (Is. XLIV. 22)"[8].

Since absolution depends on a prudent judgment of the gravity of the sins committed and of the dispositions of the penitent, it is obvious that confession of sin is necessary in a Church whose ministers have not received the miraculous gift of reading the hidden secrets of the human heart.

To be absolved, the sinner must have the proper dispositions. All through the history of the Church two conditions were required as proof of the goodwill of the penitent: contrition and satisfaction. By his act of contrition, the sinner, as far as lies in his power, revokes the pact he had made with sin and reverses the act of will by which he preferred the creature to the Creator.

Satisfaction is an essential element in true contrition. When a person sincerely repents of having disturbed the order of justice, the very sincerity of his repentance prompts him to undertake true and positive reparation.

By the folly of his sin he had smashed the internal and external harmony of the universe; his reparation consists in reassembling the shattered fragments of his life and rebuilding them into the pattern of the new creation.

In the Old Testament, contrition and satisfaction were required as necessary accompaniments of every appeal for divine pardon. The frequently used phrase "Do penance!" had a twofold implication; it included repentance and the offering of expiatory sacrifice[9].

---

[5] *Didache*, 4, 14. F. 1, 16.
[6] ibid., 14, 1, F. 1, 32.
[7] *Epistula Barnabae*, XIX, 12; *P.G.*, II, 780.
[8] *In Lucam homil.*, 17; *P.G.*, XIII, 1846.
[9] Cf. Levit., V, 5-6; III Kings, VIII, 33; I Esdras, X, 2 et seqq. where we see that penance becomes progressively more interior.

The same double theme runs through the pages of the New Testament. Everyone must ask for forgiveness of sin; everyone must accept an appropriate penance. In the course of time, a scale of penances was tabulated, and tradition has left us detailed lists of the sanctions imposed for various sins[10].

From all that has preceded, the sacrament of Penance emerges as a coherent whole, as a solidly established historical fact whose constituent elements were from the earliest ages determined by the essential purpose of the sacrament. Admittedly, the passage of time brought a development in the manner of confessing one's sins; confession was at one time made in public, whereas now it is made in the greatest secrecy.

There was also a change in the formula of absolution. During the first centuries, in both the Latin and Greek rites, absolution was granted in the form of an invocation, not in the form of a declaratory sentence (*Ego te absolvo*) as is the practice to-day. But the three essential elements did not change: confession, contrition and absolution have always been an integral part of the sacrament of Penance.

The wealth of mystery contained in this sacrament of Christian reparation gave rise to many problems. In face of these problems, faith does not remain idle, but by its own inner force it strives to win a greater degree of understanding by a deeper scrutiny of the sources of revealed truth.

Among the many questions which arise we may ask, Why is Penance so different from Baptism? Is not Baptism also a work of divine mercy? Does not Baptism also restore Divine Life which had been lost by Original Sin? Why is the sacrament of re-generation presented in the trappings of a court of justice?

Could it be that the Divine Goodness which had already granted full pardon at Baptism had somehow tired of bestowing mercy and so invented the sacrament of Penance as the sign of love that had grown less ardent? We know that this is far from the truth.

On the other hand, the emphasis laid on the acts elicited by the penitent would seem to detract from the merciful efficacy of the sacrament itself *ex opere operato*. Would it not be possible to hold that the Christian is himself the author of his rehabilitation since he contributes the essential elements of his forgiveness?

[10] The Sacramentaries of the Middle Ages have preserved lists of such penances.

These are some of the questions connected with this sacrament of the Divine Goodness. We shall seek the answers in the teaching of the Church, and here as elsewhere we shall be guided by a consideration of the Divine Life immanent in the Mystical Body of which the penitent is a member. Grace holds the key to the problem.

Firstly, let us recall a fact that is of universal application to all living things. Everything that lives bears within itself certain powers of recuperation, powers that can compensate for loss of members and loss of vital energy. It was this recuperative power of living things that gave the *vitalists* their strongest argument in favour of the transcendence of vital action over the physico-chemical forces of material being.

Though this power of self-restoration is a certain sign of imperfection in the living being, it none the less denotes a perfection of life itself in so far as it possesses the power to preserve itself in spite of the opposition that threatens the living organism.

On the supernatural plane, the Divine Life of grace which is bestowed on man in all his human weakness and instability is constantly exposed to danger—weakness, disease, even death. It is to be expected, then, that this Divine Life should also possess in itself the power to renew its strength and to undo the damage sustained in struggling against adverse conditions. And even when a soul has died in the death of sin, the sacrament of Penance performs the miracle of resurrection.

If we now consider the way in which the miracle of supernatural resurrection takes place, we shall get a better understanding of the magnificence of God's goodness as revealed in the sacrament of Penance. In bestowing the power to forgive sins on the Apostles, Our Lord was entrusting that power to His Church in perpetuity. Not that He gave every member of the Church power to absolve; the power was given to the Body as a whole to be exercised through its ordained ministers.

So we can say that the Church follows the laws of every living organism: its ailing and dead members recover life and health by a power immanent in the organism itself. The Church is a living organism possessing a divine vitality; she has the power of healing her sick members and of revitalizing those that have died.

How is this power exercised? To give a satisfactory answer to this question, we must first consider what is this Body which we call the Church and who are its members.

The Church is a social body animated by Divine Life. This Life is a real life; it is not called "life" by any mere metaphor or figure of speech. It is, like all life, an ontological principle of unity and not simply a principle of moral union such as exists between the members of a club[11]. It is also a social life, lived in common by many members who form one vital unity, one Body: *ut sint unum*. Its membership embraces a plurality of human beings each possessed of liberty and conscience.

From this it follows that the restoration of Divine Life in the individual member must be, at one and the same time, a corporate act of the whole Body and a personal act on the part of the individual. From this we can understand why the whole organism of the Church has a part to play in the spiritual restoration of its sick and dead members. She exercises her healing rôle through those members to whom she has entrusted the power of spiritual healing. At the same time it is evident that the individual member, who is a personal agent, must also contribute to his own cure.

Since here there is question of personal action, action by the moral person (the Church) and by the physical person (the sinner), it follows that the restoration of Divine Life must conform to the laws governing personal action. A person, endowed with free will and conscience, is a being who knows what he is doing and who acts by freewill. The sinner then must recognise his fault and must elicit a deliberate act of will by which he detests his sin and resolves to make satisfaction.

The Church, for her part, must know of the sin committed, and this she cannot do without a confession made by the sinner; secondly, the Church must come to a free decision as regards the remission of the sin confessed. Thus we can clearly distinguish two sets of acts, those of the penitent, which are confession, contrition and satisfaction, and those of the Church which are the passing of judgment (both on the gravity of the sin and the dispositions of the penitent) and the granting of absolution.

What is here stated in cold and formal terms is seen as something wonderfully consoling when we remember that the sinner

---

[11] Cf. The Encyclical *Mystici Corporis Christi*.

and the Church are not opposed as defendant and magistrate in a court of law; the baptised Christian, even when he has sinned, still forms part of the Church. He is one with the Church, in that vital unity which binds the members to the whole Body.

This series of actions, both on the part of the penitent and of the Church, is animated throughout by divine grace. Grace is the life of the Mystical Body, and it is grace alone that actually accomplishes the healing process. Just as it is the life of living beings that animates all their activities and gives them their vitality, so grace, the supernatural life of the Body of Christ, works in and through the activities of the members.

To illustrate this truth let us recall that in the nutritive process, for example, it is the living organism which performs the act of eating, but it is the life of the organism which assimilates the nourishment—and this assimilative process goes on without any awareness on the part of the animal. Similarly when a patient has an injury, he shows the wound to his doctor, and the latter applies a remedy; but it is the hidden power of life that turns the remedy to account and ultimately effects a cure.

Something like this happens when the sacrament of Penance heals the ailing members in the Body of the Church. It is grace and grace alone that heals, but in doing so grace acts in and through the activity of the whole Body (acting through the confessor) and the activity of the individual member who comes to seek the restoration of Divine Life.

We have mentioned the words "cure" and "healing". It is to be remarked that Catholic tradition in general frequently compares the rôle of the priest in the confessional to that of a doctor treating a patient. The judgment preceding absolution is compared to the medical diagnosis rather than to the verdict passed by a judge at the end of a courtroom trial.

Tradition does not, however, deny that the sacrament of Penance includes a judicial aspect, but it stresses the fact that the exercise of justice towards the penitent is at the same time an exercise of loving mercy. Aphraates writes:

"A man wounded in battle is not ashamed to put himself in the hands of a skilful doctor; he is not deterred by the fact that he came off second best in the battle. In the same way, a person whom Satan has struck down should not be ashamed to confess his defeat and ask for a remedial penance"[12].

St. John Chrysostom says:

"You should not be ashamed to go to a priest because you have sinned; rather this should be the motive impelling you to approach him. No one would be so foolish as to say, 'I have an ulcer and for that reason I do not want either a doctor or a cure!' On the contrary, that is the very reason why one needs both doctor and medicine"[13].

St. Jerome summarizes the Christian position in a few words:

"If a sick man is ashamed to show his wound to the doctor, medical art cannot cure what is kept concealed"[14].

In the sacrament of Penance the confessor exercises his power as judge as an integral part of the healing process. The combination of these two powers—to judge and to heal—exercised in a very human way in the confessional is in itself a revelation of the profound mystery that in God justice and love are identical.

Having determined the constituent elements of the sacrament of Penance, and having shown the meaning and scope of the various acts of penitent and priest, we must now let our minds dwell on the identification of justice and love in God and so proceed to a deeper appreciation of this particular sign of grace and try to probe the secret of the penitent's participation in the Life of the Blessed Trinity.

In the *Summa Theologica*, St. Thomas gives a lucid explanation of the special attributes of justice as it is exercised in the sacrament of Penance.

"It has been said above that reparation for an offence is made in a different way in Penance and in vindictive justice. In vindictive justice reparation is made according to the decision of the judge and not according to the will of the offending person or of the person offended; but in Penance an offence is repaired according to the will of the sinner and according to the decision of God against Whom the sin is committed. "The reason is that in this case (in Penance) it is not merely a question of restoring the equality of justice—as in vindictive justice—but rather of the restoration of

---

[12] *Demonstrationes*, VII, 3; *P.S., I*, 318.
[13] *Homiliae ineditae*, 2; *P.G., LXV*, 463.
[14] *In Ecclesiasten Commentarius*, X, 11; *P.L., XXIII*, 1096.

friendship; and this is done when the offending person makes reparation according to the will of the person whom he offended"[15].

There exists, then, a type of justice that is wholly impregnated with friendship and it is this justice which is administered in the sacrament of Penance.

St. Thomas had previously vindicated this point of view by excluding from Penance the idea of rigid vindictive justice. This latter is possible only when there is equality between the persons concerned; whereas in Penance there is question of restoring order between servant and master, between son and father, between husband and spouse[16].

It follows from this that mercy alone can supply what strict justice is incapable of effecting.

The inequality existing between the persons concerned, while excluding the possibility of strict vindictive justice, opens the way for an outpouring of love in which God treats us as His servants, His children, His spouse. What is an apparent rift in the order of justice reveals the Divine pity in all its splendour, and in the exercise of the Divine mercy we see the full expression of the Divine justice.

Justice, in effect, is nothing more or less than the integrity of right order. And order means the proper relation of all things to God. But God is love. Hence it follows that perfect justice will be a work of love and he alone will be justified who is integrated into the order of Divine Love.

Love of sinners, as love of the poor and the sick, will express itself in the removal of their ills, the cure of their sickness, the alleviation of their poverty. Love of sinners will always be a love full of mercy.

The sacrament of Penance was instituted to restore the order of justice, which, as we have just seen, is at the same time an order of merciful love. God, priest and sinner meet in the confessional; the God, Whose grace is full of mercy, the priest who raises up

---

[15] " Dictum est autem supra (q. 85, a. 3, ad 3) quod alio modo fit recompensatio offensae in poenitentia et in vindicativa justitia. Nam in vindicativa justitia fit recompensatio secundum arbitrium judicis, non secundum voluntatem offendentis vel offensi; sed in poenitentia fit recompensatio offensae secundum voluntatem peccantis et secundum arbitrium Dei in quem peccatur; quia hic non quaeritur sola redintegratio aequalitatis justitiae, sicut in justitia vindicativa; sed magis reconciliatio amicitiae quod fit dum offendens recompensat secundum voluntatem ejus quem offendit." (*S. Th.*, III, q. 90, a. 2, c).

[16] ibid, q. 85, a. 3, c.

the sinner in the name of the Church, and the sinner himself whose response to the divine invitation consists in an act of the love of God which is also an act of mercy towards his own soul.

We have said that justice is fulfilled in mercy. There is a prayer in the Sacramentary of Gelasius which shows how the Christians of the 7th century understood this blending of divine justice and divine liberality in the sacrament of Penance.

"May he escape the terrors of darkness and the agony of fire, and, turning back from the path of error to the way of justice, may he never again suffer fresh wounds but rather may he preserve whole and inviolate that which thy grace has bestowed and thy mercy restored"[18].

We find the same idea expressed in the *De Penitentia* of Halitgarius, Bishop of Cambrai, who states that justice is the fountainhead (*de justitiae fonte*) from which flow liberality, benevolence and charity[19].

The harmony of justice and mercy in the sacrament of Penance is in itself a revelation of the Life of the Father and of the Son and of the Holy Ghost. Like every work of divine love, the sacrament of divine mercy reveals the ineffable secret of the Godhead: God is love. Supernatural revelation alone puts us in possession of the secret of a love existing in God by which His Being surges eternally, in an infinite act of love within the Godhead.

God cannot be other than Three Divine Persons Who give themselves in mutual and eternal love within the bosom of perfect unity. To the eye of faith every external work of divine love is a participation in the intra-Trinitarian love of God and bears a reflex of the eternal and mutual giving of the Three Divine Persons within the Blessed Trinity.

The sacrament of Penance reveals the life of the Divine Persons more emphatically than any other work of the Divine Goodness. It reveals the reaction of the Blessed Trinity to sin, and specifically to the sin of the prodigal son.

---

[17] The date of the Sacramentary attributed to Pope Gelasius is uncertain. It is commonly admitted that it belongs to the 6th or 7th century.

[18] " Nesciat quod terret in tenebris, quod stridet in flammis atque ab erroris via ad iter reversus justitiae nequaquam ultra novis vulneribus sauciatur, sed integrum sit ei atque perpetuum et quod gratia tua contulit et quod misericordia reformavit." (*Sacrament. Gelas.*, Lib. I, 38; *P.L.*, LXXIV, 1097).

[19] *Le Poenitent.*, Lib. II, cap. VIII; *P.L.*, C.V. 675.

Let it be remarked that God would still be a God of love even if He did not go so far as to forgive sin over and over again. The creation of the world was an act of love. Man's gratuitous elevation to the supernatural plane was a much greater manifestation of divine love. The Redemption achieved through the Incarnation of the Only Begotten Son added the plenitude of divine mercy to the gratuitous gifts which God in His love had already bestowed on man.

The other sacraments and the liturgical life of the Church are so many channels through which the Divine Persons dispense the treasures of merciful love. Yes, if one were to imagine Christianity without the sacrament of Penance it would still be a religion of love and pardon.

It would lack, however, an adequate expression of the measure of the divine mercy—which is to bestow mercy beyond all measure; it would lack the "seventy times seven times" of the Gospel, which is a measure of forgiveness inconceivable to mere man who considers sevenfold pardon a very liberal standard[20].

Faced with the accumulation of repeated sins of ingratitude and infidelity and treachery, such a Christianity would not reveal the permanent reaction of God's love which takes up the shattered remnants with which our path is strewn and reconstructs them into a work of divine justice which is also a masterpiece of divine love.

It is here that the sacrament of Penance introduces a completely new element into the story of God's dealings with man. Having loved him already to excess, God gives man the sacrament of Penance as an abiding manifestation of the love of the Father, Son and Holy Ghost, a love so exceeding great that with every repetition of the words of pardon the Three Divine Persons give Themselves to the repentant sinner.

Our forgiveness comes from the Father, Son and Holy Ghost; or, more correctly, it comes from the Father, through the Son and in the Spirit of their mutual love. Divine love first proceeds from the Father, Who in God is the origin derived from no other origin. Source of light and life, He is also the source of love and of love in all its manifestations.

From the Person of the Father springs mercy and pardon; He it is Who has sent His Son to save the world. But the divine love

---

[20] Matthew. XVIII, 21-23.

and pity and forgiveness also belong to the Son Who is the living and perfect image of the Father. Every throb of Divine Life originating in the Father pulsates eternally in the Son Who is born of the Father's substance.

Thus it is that all goodness and paternity are revealed to the world through the Son. The Son is the revelation of the Father. Further, it is through the Son that the merciful goodness of the Father continues to operate in the world because it is the Son Who has organized the ministry of pardon in His Church. He is the Mediator between the Father and mankind and through Him the pardon of the Father is extended to sinners of all generations; through Him, likewise, the sinner is reconciled with his Heavenly Father.

Finally, we are pardoned in the Holy Ghost. If we had remained ignorant of the fact that the Holy Ghost proceeds from the Father and the Son as from a single principle (*tanquam ab uno principio*), the gift of the Holy Ghost might appear as a divine superfluity. Since we already possess everything through the Son, is it not superfluous to assert that we must receive the same divine plenitude in the Holy Ghost?

In reality, the revelation that in God there is a community of Persons and that the Father and the Son are a single principle whence the Holy Ghost proceeds throws a new light on the ineffable mystery of God's love. Just as the Father and the Son cannot communicate their being within the Trinity without the Holy Ghost proceeding as their mutual and subsistent Love, so they cannot communicate themselves externally to us without sending us their Holy Spirit. They dwell in us only through the gift of the Holy Ghost.

When the Father and the Son bestow their gifts of light and forgiveness on sinners, when they give us a share in their Personal Life, they do so only in the Holy Ghost. Since He is the eternal expression of their mutual love, every work of divine love on earth, every communication of a Divine Person necessarily takes place *in* the Holy Spirit.

Hence we can understand that the work of redemption which began with the sending of the Son is completed by the gift of the Spirit. If we do not possess within us the Spirit of the Divine Community, we cannot belong to that Community; but once we possess Him we are admitted to close union with the Father and the Son.

From all this it becomes clear how the sacrament of Penance is the work of the whole Trinity. Here as in all the sacraments the Christian must be conformed to Christ if he is to receive the full fruits and the full efficacy of the sacrament. Christ the Redeemer is come to save that which was lost[21].

The purpose of all His preaching and all His ministry on earth was to reveal and establish a ministry of mercy by which sinners would be cured of their sickness and the dead restored to life. The penitent Christian who goes to confession conforms himself to the Divine Healer and conforms his will to the Will of Christ by choosing to turn from sin and death and to rise again to newness of life in Christ.

By conformity with Christ in and through His Sacred Humanity, the Christian becomes conformed to the Divine Person of the Word of Whom the psalmist said, "Sacrifice and oblation thou wouldst not, but a body thou hast fitted for me"[22].

Conformed to the Word of God, the Christian is brought into intimate union with the Father in the Holy Ghost. The prodigal son is restored to the bosom of the Father of mercies Who embraces him in the joy of the Spirit of love.

This is no mere figure of speech. It is the tremendous reality summed up in those words which ceaselessly announce the message of divine goodness in our sinful world: *Ego te absolvo in nomine Patris et Filii et Spiritus Sancti. Amen.*

---

[21] Luke, XIX, 10.

[22] Ps. XXXIX, 7.

CHAPTER VI

MATRIMONY

MARRIAGE as a sacrament signifies and effects a conformity between the wedded couple and Christ. This poses a problem that at first sight appears insoluble. Christ was a virgin and many times in the Gospel we read of His preference for the state of virginity. How, then, can we discover any degree of conformity between a married couple and the Master Whom the Church invokes as "Jesu, corona virginum—Jesus, crown of virgins"?

St. Paul offers a solution to the problem. Christ has chosen a spouse, the Church, Mother of all the faithful. According to the theology of St. Paul, married Christians are called to mirror forth in their own lives the life of union that exists between Christ and the Church. Thereby they participate in the redemptive and sanctifying rôle of Christ in the world and they receive in their souls a special share in the Divine Life of grace.

Husband and wife belong to each other and in this they resemble Christ and the Church; by grace, they actually participate in the union between Christ and His Spouse. To elucidate this truth, we shall consider the various elements in the sacrament of Matrimony in the light of the mutual gift of self that takes place between Christ and the Church.

In this way we hope to emphasize the truth that Matrimony is a sacrament only because it signifies this mystical union, which of itself gives a new meaning and a new perfection to all the values involved in the matrimonial contract between Christians.

In conclusion, by considering the union that binds Christ to His Church, we shall see Christian marriage as a new participation in the life of the Blessed Trinity Whose splendour transforms conjugal society into a thing of divine beauty and supernatural dignity.

To begin, let us recall a basic fact of Church law. Canon 1012, § 2 of the Code of Canon Law states that between baptized persons there is no valid marriage except the sacrament of Matrimony. This categorical statement of the Christian position marks the end of a long period of controversy.

In the 17th century, Marcus Ant. de Dominis[1] held that since the sacrament of Matrimony added something to the natural contract, it could also be separated from it. This theory reappeared in the writings of J. Launoy[2] and was revived by J. Nuyts in the 19th century.[3]

One consequence of this position was that it accorded the civil power the right to determine marriage impediments; a more serious effect was that it modified the traditional concept as to what exactly constituted the essential elements of the sacrament. These latter, according to the Catholic view, are determined by the necessary elements of the contract itself; the natural contract and the wills of the contracting parties constitute the matter, form and minister of the sacrament.

In this respect Matrimony is unique among the sacraments, as was well understood by Melchior Cano when he proposed a compromise solution. He affirmed that the contract itself constituted the matter of the sacrament, but that the form consisted in the blessing of the marriage by the assisting priest. Hence, if the blessing were omitted, the marriage would still be valid as a contract, but it would not be a sacrament.[4]

The position of Vasquez was still more uncertain. He agreed that the contract and the sacrament were identical, but he held that the contracting parties could make an act of will by which they excluded the sacramental nature of the marriage and thus reduced it to the level of a merely natural contract.

As against these various attempts to separate the sacrament from the marriage contract, the opinion of St. Thomas prevailed[5]. In the allocution *Acerbissimum vobiscum*, Pope Pius IX declared that between the faithful there could be no matrimonial contract which was not also a sacrament[6]. Thirty years later, Pope Leo XIII

---

[1] *De Republica Christiana*, 1. III et IV, c. 2.

[2] *De regia in matrim. poteste*, t. 1, p. 2, c. 4.

[3] Pope Pius IX condemned the following proposition: " Matrimonii sacramentum non est nisi quid contractui accessorium ab eoque separabile, ipsumque sacramentum in una tantum nuptiali benedictione situm est ". (*Syllabus*, prop. 66; Denz. 1766).

[4] *De locis theol.*, 1. VIII, c. 5.

[5] *Supplementum*, q. 45, a. 1, c.

[6] Denz., 1640.

repeated the same assertion: the sacrament cannot be separated from the contract since the contract itself is the sacrament.

Nothing is more at variance with the truth than to regard the sacrament as an extra adornment (*decus quoddam adjunctum*) and a superadded extrinsic quality (*proprietatem illapsam extrinsecus*) which the contracting parties could dissociate from the contract itself. In a word, Pope Leo XIII condemned the position held by Vasquez[7].

In developing this teaching, the Pope relied on the concept of marriage that is traditional in the Church and which derives from the Epistle to the Ephesians[8]. The sacrament of Matrimony is not a new creation; it consists in the elevation of the primitive marriage contract to the supernatural order.

By its original institution, the marriage contract consists in the mutual donation of self that takes place between man and woman. This doctrine, which has now been inscribed in the Code of Canon Law, bears the theological note of " certain " (*certum*): between baptized persons the only valid marriage contract is the sacrament of Matrimony.

Is the significance of the sacrament—the union of Christ and the Church—a matter of equal certitude? There is no doubt that the union existing between Christ and the Church is the perfect exemplar of Christian marriage. This is a truth contained in Holy Scripture. St. Paul regards Matrimony as a great sacrament because it resembles the life of union and the mutual donation of self that exists between Christ and the Church[9].

But does this assimilation of Matrimony to the union of Christ and the Church constitute the essence of the sacrament? The very notion of a sacrament would seem to give rise to an insurmountable difficulty. A sacrament produces the grace which it signifies. Matrimony may well signify the union between Christ and the Church, but it by no means causes that union.

In what way, then, does Matrimony verify the fundamental conditions of every sacrament? In what way is it an efficacious sign of grace?

---

[7] *Arcanum divinae sapientiae*, Denz., 1853.
[8] Ephes., V, 22-32.
[9] ibid.

St. Thomas raises the question in the *Summa Theologica,* but the answer he gives is somewhat evasive[10]. Admittedly, he says, the union between Christ and the Church is not contained but only signified in Matrimony. That union is outside the scope of sacramental causality. But there is something else which is both contained and signified in the sacrament of Matrimony, namely, the grace to live and act in harmony with the final end of marriage[11].

According to this view, we are forced to conclude (and St. Thomas, following the Master of the Sentences, seems to have adopted the conclusion), that we have two realities signified in the sacrament of Matrimony. The first is immanent in the sacrament and consists in divine grace and all the actual help necessary to attain the end of marriage; the other is transcendent and is nothing less than the union between Christ and the Church.

If, however, one has regard to the teaching of St. Paul, especially his doctrine of the Mystical Body, one can without difficulty conclude that both the realities signified in the sacrament of Matrimony bear an intrinsic relation to each other and they fuse together in the one great reality which is the Church.

The special grace of Matrimony is a grace that unites two baptized persons, that is, two members of the Mystical Body. This union cannot possibly take place except by virtue of the union existing between Christ, the Head, and His Church (which is the origin of every communication of grace to the faithful).

The union between Christ and the Church is not extrinsic to the sacrament of Matrimony; it is necessarily involved in it. Furthermore, one can say in a very real sense that the union of Christians in marriage, since it consists formally in the donation of one member of the Mystical Body to another, strengthens the bond between Christ and His Church.

The reason for saying this is that the matrimonial union of Christians is effected in Christ and in the Church and its effect is an increase of grace in the whole Body through the new influx of Divine Life into two of Its members.

Hence, we can say without error that Matrimony *does* produce

---

[10] Supplem. 47, 1. obj. 4.
[11] ibid. ad 4 et ad 5, et art. 2 in c.
[12] Cf. Ephes., IV, 1-16; I Cor., XII, 4-31; Rom., XII, 3. Writing to the Ephesians St. Paul reminds them that Christ is " edified " by the growth of all the members of His Body.

the grace which it signifies by strengthening the union between the Church and Christ. It does not cause the initial union between Christ and His Spouse, but it brings that union to a new degree of perfection.

This interpretation is not formally contained in the text of the Epistle to the Ephesians; but the text in which St. Paul speaks of Christian marriage should not be taken in isolation from the whole doctrinal scheme of which it forms part. Since St. Paul states that the union between Christ and the Church is signified in Christian marriage, it is evident that the doctrinal background to his treatment of marriage is his teaching on the Mystical Body.

According to this teaching, Christ is immanent in the Church and He takes possession of the activity of each member and makes it contribute to the good of the whole Body. Likewise, through the activity of the individual members whom He has incorporated into His Mystical Body, the whole Christ grows in stature and fulfilment.

In the light of this teaching, we can conclude without fear of exaggeration that Christian Matrimony is not only a symbol of the union between Christ and the Church; it is a real participation in that union and it strengthens the bond uniting the members with the Head.

Once this is admitted, the Catholic teaching on Christian marriage appears resplendent with divine light and beauty. It suffices to keep one's gaze turned towards the mystical union existing between Christ and the Church to discern the full supernatural import of this most natural of all unions, the marital union of husband and wife.

Firstly, it is clear that the union between Christ and the Church, prototype of Christian marriage, is effected by a mutual surrender of each to the other. Christ not only delivered Himself to His enemies in order to give life to the Church; He also delivered Himself and continues to deliver Himself to the Church.

To her He gives Himself completely, His Body and Blood, His Person as Word Incarnate with all the graces that flow from the Incarnation; all this He gives to the Church so that in His Name she can absolve and consecrate and anoint, and that thus the whole Christ, Head and members, may be ceaselessly offered up to the Father.

On her side, the Church continually offers herself to the Lord, giving Him her body with all its members, and uniting in that oblation all the earthly things which she sanctifies, all the good thoughts and deeds and desires of her members, so that she may become more intimately one with her Divine Spouse and He with her.

Between Christ and the Church there is a reciprocal surrender of self, which is an image of the reciprocity that should exist between husband and wife from the very beginning of their life together. Each gives the other the right over his or her body; each yields up what belongs to self and enters into possession of what belongs to the other; each partner lives for the other, each lives in the other.

Here we have perfect similarity with the intimate union between Christ and the Church, a union so close that it becomes a mutual immanence. Christ lives in the Church and the Church in Christ. In marriage, there is a surrender of the body which implies that two lives, two persons, have fused in one.

This surrender has no value, however, unless it is freely made. Just as Christ gave Himself freely to the Church (and He does not accept any offering that is not freely made), so, too, the mutual free consent of bride and groom constitutes the very essence of the matrimonial contract. Their consent is by definition an interior act, but it is manifested externally by unmistakable signs of self-donation.

If we consider the end of marriage, we find a further degree of conformity between the union of husband and wife and the union of Christ and the Church. Christian tradition maintains that the primary end of marriage is the procreation and education of children; secondarily, marriage is instituted for the mutual help and support of husband and wife so that they may have the strength to fulfil all the duties and face all the difficulties of married life.

The union between Christ and the Church has exactly the same end. For why did Christ institute the Church? Why did He institute it as His Mystical Body? His purpose was that through the Church He might generate Christians to newness of life and educate them in that life which flows from the bosom of the Eternal Father.

As we have already indicated, the Son is charged with the distribution of the Divine Life that derives from the Father. Since, however, this Divine Life has to be communicated to men, Christ has ordained that they should receive It as the gift of a mother.

In the natural order, men come to life by being born of a mother. God respects this natural order and so He has ordained that in the supernatural order, too, men will find the means of salvation and sanctification at a mother's breast, and draw Divine Life from the tenderness of a mother's love. It follows from this that the primary end of the union of Christ with His Church is the generation and education of sons of God.

Since Christ chooses to use The Church in the work of salvation, we may say that to achieve this primary end which governs all the modalities of their reciprocal intimacy, it is essential that Christ and the Church should constantly aid each other. As a wife finds strength in her husband, so the Church draws strength from Christ. She could not win the slightest success in her mission on earth were she not assured of the permanent efficacy of her reliance on Christ.

Almost 2,000 years of struggle amid triumph and defeat have strengthened her grasp of the truth of Christ's words, "Without Me you can do nothing". She is keenly aware that without complete surrender of herself to Christ her every effort is vain and every hope an illusion.

On the other hand, is there any campaign of spiritual conquest, or grace, or hope of salvation which can come to fulfilment without The Church? Is it not she who gives Christ the minds and hearts and limbs of her members without whose co-operation nothing would be undertaken, must less completed, with a view to establishing the Kingdom of God?

Does she not every day offer Christ the sweat and suffering and death of a countless host of hidden martyrs so that the Passion of the Head may be made manifest in the passion of His members?

In Christian marriage, too, the secondary end of mutual help and consolation, though subordinate to the primary end, is none the less important; it is essential for the attainment of the primary end—the procreation and education of children. The union between Christ and the Church, and their mutual trust and reliance, is the perfect archetype and the living example of the mutual self-surrender of husband and wife.

The sacrament of Matrimony bears fruit in a whole series of

graces that derives ultimately from the grace of union existing between Christ and the Church; graces of love and strength that help husband and wife to bear the burden of their common life; graces of generosity that culminate in the heroism of the gift of new life; grace to face any problem, to undertake any effort, to surmount any difficulty in their life of union.

Keeping in mind the subordination of ends, which is the guiding principle in the direction and organization of all life, we must conclude that Christian Matrimony wonderfully mirrors forth the mystery of Christ in His constant self-oblation to the Church, and the mystery of the Church in her total consecration to Christ.

After considering the ends of marriage, we shall now examine the properties that characterize Christian Matrimony. Here we shall find more explicit expression of the similarity that exists between the married life of Christians and the life shared by Christ and the Church.

Marriage is, firstly, indissoluble. Is not the Church indissolubly and forever united to Christ? Marriage is exclusive of all other partnership. It must be so since it is a symbol of the unity between the one and only Christ and the one and only true Church.

Among the arguments brought forward in favour of monogamy there is usually an appeal to extrinsic reasons, such as the difficulty involved in bringing up children properly in a polygamous household. Such arguments are indeed important. But should one not rather seek the profound reason for the institution of monogamy in the very essence of the marriage union itself which Christ has raised to the dignity of a sacrament?

If one admits that the union of husband and wife is the image of the union of Christ and the Church, it is evident that as long as both partners are alive their lives are ruled by an exclusive dedication of each to the other. Just as there is but One Mystical Body of Christ (a truth which justifies the dictum—"no salvation outside the Church"), so we assert that a man can have only one wife who, in the language of St. Paul, becomes as it were the body of her husband.

The unity and indissolubility of marriage are inevitable in the light of the mystery which marriage signifies and from which it draws supernatural efficacy. The same divine prototype, the union of Christ and the Church, throws a revealing light on the problem of the constituent elements of the sacrament—what is the matter and the form of this sacrament?

Many theological writers have been almost paralysed with hesitancy in tackling the problem. At first sight, the thesis proposed by Melchior Cano seems the most acceptable because it appears to safeguard the analogy between Matrimony and the other sacraments better than any alternative opinion.

According to Cano, the matter consists in the contract while the form is supplied by the blessing uttered by the priest when he says *"Ego vos conjungo in matrimonium."* This explanation makes the priest the minister of the sacrament, which seems logical and in perfect accord with the practice followed in the other sacraments, where the ordinary minister is a priest or bishop.

In spite of this, Melchior Cano is at variance with the common teaching of the Church which affirms that the nuptial contract itself is both matter, and form and that the contracting parties are the minister of the sacrament to each other. This may seem a strange teaching, but it is the only explanation which fully conforms to the inner logic of the situation. Christian marriage, in a word, is a natural function ordained by God for the propagation of human life and elevated to the supernatural plane as a Christian function.

In raising marriage to the level of a sacrament, was there any need to change the slightest detail of the valid natural contract by which two human beings bind themselves with a view to the propagation of the species? Was there any need to add some extrinsic element to complete the natural marriage union?

No, there was no question of adding anything; all that was required was that the whole human content of the natural contract should be supernaturalized and christianized; all that was included in the primitive natural contract remains unchanged, but it is now elevated to the supernatural plane and charged with supernatural efficacy.

At this point we may ask, "What exactly *is* included in the matrimonial contract by virtue of its primitive institution on the natural plane?"

The contract includes the surrender by each partner and the

---

[14] Ephes., V, 28.

acceptance by the other of the right over his or her body with a view to acts that are of themselves apt for the generation of children. This mutual surrender and acceptance are expressed either in words or symbolic acts.

In the natural marriage contract thus described, we can detect the elements which determine the matter and form of the sacrament. Firstly, there is the right of one partner over the body of the other; the whole contract is organized in view of this exchange of rights.

In the sacrament of Matrimony, the right over the body of the other partner is the remote matter; the surrender and acceptance of this right must be expressed in a sense-perceptible manner. The most common interpretation is that the expression of the mutual surrender of rights constitutes the proximate matter of the sacrament, and the mutual acceptance of rights constitutes the form.

These constituent elements of the natural marriage contract are raised to the supernatural order and this can only be done if Christ and the Church, Mother of all the faithful, make the marriage contract a specifically Christian thing. This they do in the first instance in the sacrament of Baptism which makes the two partners members of Christ and of the Church in such wise that their every activity concerns Christ and the Church.

Secondly, the natural marriage contract, source of human life, is directly transformed into something that has supernatural value and meaning. The supernatural character of Christian marriage does not consist merely in the fact that husband and wife, in the state of grace, perform acts that are good and meritorious and supernaturally efficacious, but in something much more profound. Since the foundation of the Church, the generation of children according to the flesh has become the source of the life and the guarantee of the continued existence of the Church itself. Without the marriage of its members, the Church could not maintain the generation of new members of Christ to take the place of those who die.

Considering the nature and rôle of the Church, we can see a certain necessity in the establishment within her fold of the marriage contract which thus becomes the one and only source of both human and Christian life. To meet this necessity, Christ raised the natural source of human life to the level of a sacrament. He did this by vesting the marriage contract with a supernatural character, taking it to Himself, giving it a new meaning, and blessing it with a series of special graces.

Christian marriage was henceforth to be a participation in Christ's union with His ever-fruitful Spouse, the Church. It was to be intimately associated with the mystery of Christ in the Church as the indispensable condition for the continuance of that mystery; and in this sense it was to be a sacrament in the fullest meaning of the word, *signum rei sacrae*—the sign of something sacred.

The various elements of the natural contract, assumed by Christ and the Church to fulfil a sacramental rôle, become the constituent elements of the sacrament itself; likewise, the contracting parties, by their free consent and mutual exchange or rights, become the ministers of the sacrament. It is they who make the contract. It is they who in Christ and through Christ are the ministers of the sacrament to each other.

So that all this may be validly expressed and clearly ratified, the Church deputes her official witness, the priest, to bestow her maternal blessing on those children whom she brought forth to Divine Life in Baptism and to whom she now entrusts the mission of furnishing new members for her Mystical Body.

One can well understand the exclamation with which St. Paul closes his treatment of the excellence and duties of Christian marriage, "This is a great mystery, but I speak in Christ and in the Church"[15].

It is indeed a great mystery because the sacrament of Matrimony shares in the splendour of the Mystical Body itself, which in turn is a reflex of the eternal effulgence of the Divine Family of the Three Persons Who are one God.

Christian marriage like the other sacraments opens up a new avenue of approach to the Life of the Blessed Trinity; it comes from the Trinity and it leads to a fuller participation in the Life of the Three Divine Persons.

Did not Christ found the Church so that in it and through it He might bring souls to share in the Life of the Triune God? It was to reveal this Life that He became Incarnate.

Did He not say that those who saw Him saw the Father and did He not announce that He with the Father would send the Holy

---

[15] Ephes., V, 32.

Ghost upon the disciples? By His Death and Resurrection, He communicated the Life of the Blessed Trinity to the world. The end of the whole redemptive process and the special end of His Resurrection is the indwelling of the Blessed Trinity in the Church and in every soul in the state of grace.

The society which He founded was from the beginning, and by the express Will of its Founder, wholly impregnated with the Life of the Divine Society of the Father, Son and Holy Ghost. The Church is in fact a visible expression of the inner Life of God since the Life of grace that pulsates in the Mystical Body is a participation and a manifestation of the intra-Trinitarian Life of God.

Behind all the more immediate meanings of the life of the Church we must always see this primary and essential meaning which alone gives external value to all that the Church undertakes during her temporal existence on earth.

Christian marriage, as an integral part of the life of the Church, must also be considered in the light of its ultimate meaning. As we have seen, Matrimony signifies the union of Christ and the Church, that union which is the principle of all divine fecundity on earth. Through the union of Christ and His Spouse the eternal fecundity of the Father bears fruit in the generation of children of God on earth.

Consequently married Christians, sharing in the union of Christ and the Church, are brought into a special relation of conformity with the Eternal Father, the First Person of the Blessed Trinity. Both together, husband and wife, form one moral person, and even though their union does not reach the point of absolute physical identity, they come as near to it as possible in the flesh: they are "two in one flesh" and as such they form a single principle of fecundity.

In this they are an image of the eternal Father to Whom belongs the exclusive attribute of being the Source of Life within the Trinity by way of generation.

Husband and wife are one, but the purpose of their union is the production of a third person, the child, since, as we have already seen, the primary end of marriage is the procreation of children. The unity of the parents as a single principle of life issues in duality—parents and child. And straightaway we have the terrestrial trinity completed.

For the act of generation, which poses the distinction between parents and children, is also the origin of a new spirit, the spirit of family love that unites parents and children, just as in God the divine relations of paternity and filiation issue in the Holy Spirit of their mutual love.

Thus in its primary end—the union of husband and wife for the procreation of children—Christian marriage expresses a vital conformity with the Blessed Trinity.

Let us now turn to the secondary end, which presupposes the primary end to such a degree that the antecedent and irremediable incapacity of either partner to posit those acts which in their nature are apt for procreation renders a marriage null and void. In its secondary end, too, Matrimony establishes a further degree of conformity between husband and wife and the mystery of the Personal Life of the Trinity.

By the harmony of their life together, the married couple constitute a single moral person whose prototype is the eternal Father, the *Genitor,* and throughout all the phases of their married life the mutual aid which husband and wife render each other welds them into that unique society in which a duality of persons expresses the attributes of One Divine Person, the Father.

The resemblance which the sacrament of Matrimony effects between Christian married life and the mystery of the Trinity helps us to understand the two great properties of Christian marriage—its exclusiveness and its indissolubility. Christian marriage excludes all other partners. It cannot be otherwise if, as we have seen, husband and wife form but one moral person whose perfect archetype is the eternal Father.

Secondly, marriage is indissoluble and this is immediately explained by reference to the Family on which the human family is modelled, namely, the Family of the Blessed Trinity wherein Three Persons are indissolubly united in the most absolute unity, the unity of one and the same Divine Nature.

But even considering conjugal society in itself, we are forced to accept indissolubility as an inherent condition because the married partners in the union of one flesh form together a single moral person.

The Sacrament of Matrimony not only in its primary and secondary ends, not only in its properties, but also in its fruits, signifies and contains a series of graces whose purpose is to perfect the participation of the members of the human family in the inner Life of the Three Divine Persons, graces whose effect is to produce an intensely vital conformity between the human family and the Family of the eternal Three.

These are actual graces of light and strength; grace to be always an effective principle of life—and this extends beyond the act of generation to the upbringing and education of children; grace that will enable parents and children together to promote that spirit of family love which will be an image of the Holy Spirit proceeding from the Father and the Son.

In view of all this, we can understand that marriage, which heretics have considered either as intrinsically evil or at best a necessary evil to be tolerated on account of human weakness (*ad duritiam cordis*), is really what Catholic tradition has always asserted it to be—the efficacious sign of the most sublime of all mysteries. For it is by marriage that humanity in its primitive constitution expresses an astonishing resemblance with the mystery of the Blessed Trinity.

Even within the limits of the purely natural contract, marriage establishes a relation of similarity between man and God. Through the conjugal union, man becomes the father of a person who is also man, and this generation in the flesh is an image of the inner mystery of the Trinity in which God is the Father of a Person who is also God.

Raised to the dignity of a sacrament, Christian marriage institutes a more sublime relation between man and God, since it makes the partners in marriage participate in the mystery of the divine processions.

All creation is the work of the Blessed Trinity and in one way or other bears the trace of its Triune Creator; in every work of God there is some expression of the mystery of the Three Persons Who are one God. Within the scheme of created things, the function of preserving the human race by marriage bears a striking resemblance to the inner mystery of the Trinity.

But just as the revelation made by Christ while on earth is the only source of our knowledge that the world was created by a

Trinity of Persons, so too it is only since Christ raised the marriage contract to the dignity of a sacrament that Christian married life has become an intimate sharing in the Divine Life of the Blessed Trinity.

Christ alone, the universal and perfect Mediator between God and man, has given marriage this sublime dignity. For this reason, Matrimony as an efficacious sign of grace must signify something in Christ, namely, His union with the Church, a union which in its own way is a symbol of the greatest of all unions, that existing eternally between the Three Persons in God.

Christ renewed the original marriage institution not by adding a new contract to supplement the natural contract nor by adding some element to perfect the existing one. Rather, Christ took the divinely instituted natural marriage contract and gave it a higher mode of existence, raising it to the supernatural order and making it a real participation in the Divine Life.

By this sublimation, marriage and married life are no longer a mere created image, however perfect, of the Blessed Trinity; they have become through the life of grace an actual participation in the inner Life of the Trinity.

The life of grace animating all aspects of conjugal and family life finds expression in a spirit of supernatural love that transcends mere human love and which is a participation in the Holy Spirit Who is Christ's gift to all Christian spouses: *Apud vos manebit et in vobis erit*[16].

It seems clear, then, that Christian marriage, blossoming into full family life, affords one of the most accessible approaches to an appreciation of the first and greatest of all mysteries. We seek far and wide, and often in vain, for images and comparisons that will help the faithful to get a little closer to the mystery of Three Persons in One God. Perhaps we are blind to the obvious.

The father and mother of a family will find no more perfect created expression of the Trinity than the wonders of their own family life. The close unity that exists between parents and children is vastly inferior to the unity existing in God; no created unity can ever approach the unity of Three Persons in one identical Nature.

---

[16] John, XIV, 17.

But the unity of the Christian family is a reality that should be pondered by all the members of the family. It consists in the life of parents and children together, a community of life based on generation, a life that develops in a spirit of mutual understanding and reciprocal love that rises in the hearts of both parents and children.

Are we not justified, then, in saying that Christian family life, initiated by the sacrament of Matrimony provides the most obvious approach to a deeper appreciation of the mystery of the Blessed Trinity?

CHAPTER VII

HOLY ORDERS

IN THE EPISTLE to the Hebrews, St. Paul speaks of the priest as a mediator. He is a pontiff "Taken from among men in the things that appertain to God that he may offer up gifts and sacrifices for sins; who can have compassion on them that are ignorant and that err ".[1] The priesthood is a bond of union between man and God.

These revealing words of the Apostle give an immediate grasp of the universal scope of the priestly office. The priesthood is instituted to bring all mankind into union with God by a ministry of reconciliation, and with mankind to reconcile the whole world to the Creator.

To enable us to advance some degree in the understanding of the mystery of this sacrament of union, we must first consider the One Great High-Priest, Jesus Christ, True God become true man at the Incarnation. He is the perfect bond between Heaven and Earth. By considering Jesus in the whole sweep of His redemptive action and in the full exercise of His priesthood on earth, we shall see exemplified in the highest degree every aspect of the Christian priesthood. What, then, is Jesus Christ?

Christ is Life[2] and the source of Life[3]; He is the Truth[4] and He is the Light[5]; He is the Way[6] and He is also the Shepherd Who leads His flock to the Father[7]. This triple aspect of His ministry among us, a ministry of life and guidance, includes in itself the many aspects of the priestly ministry exercised by the Church according to the various grades of the hierarchy.

Though it is a varied ministry, the priesthood is ever and always

---

[1] Hebrews, V. 1-2.
[2] John, I, 4; XI, 25-26.
[3] John, IV, 10-14; VI, 35-60.
[4] ibid. XIV, 6.
[5] ibid. VIII, 12.
[6] ibid. XIV, 6.
[7] John, X, 14, 27.

engaged in pursuing its essential function as a bond of union, ever devoted to achieving the three great unities—*unity of life* in the dispensation of divine life here below; *unity of thought* by bringing the minds of men into harmony with the one Truth; and *unity of will* by bringing the hearts of men into conformity with the love of God and leading them along the way to the Father.

This concept of Holy Orders coincides with the concept of the hierarchy considered in its diverse manifestations and in the full scope of its activity. It includes much more than is contained within the strict limits of the sacrament of Holy Orders, which, strictly speaking, is limited to the power of offering sacrifice and sanctifying the world by the administration of the sacraments.

In adopting this broader point of view, we may seem to be going beyond the scope of the present work, but we prefer not to separate elements which indeed are distinct but which, by the Will of Christ, Founder of the Church, have been fused into close union. Undoubtedly, a priest is really a priest, even if he never preaches, and even if he has not received the power of jurisdiction; similarly, a bishop may exercise jurisdiction before he has received the episcopal consecration.

But the priesthood does not attain the full measure of priestly action without a share in the jurisdiction and preaching ministry of the Church, and on the other hand, the exercise of jurisdiction cannot fulfil its rôle of feeding the flock of Christ without the power of the sacrament of Holy Orders.

To sanctify, to instruct and to guide are the three essential functions of the Redeemer and they are equally essential functions in that Church which was founded to prolong the presence and redemptive action of Christ among us. All three functions blend together in the exercise of Holy Orders and make of the priest another Christ—*alter Christus.*

Let no one be surprised if we do not lay special emphasis on the distinction between the three powers; no Catholic would think of denying that they are distinct. But while it would be false to identify them (as the Protestants did), it would be disastrous for the life of the Church to separate them and to regard them as isolated and self-sufficient entities rather than as distinct but complementary aspects of the same priestly hierarchy.

Holy Orders is a sacrament whose function is to achieve unity.

1. *Unity of life.*

The most important function of the priesthood is to bring the sanctity of God into contact with the world. In the communication of the divine sanctity to mankind, the world finds a new and perfect form of unity since it enters into the divine communion and shares in the life of the one God. United to God by sharing in the Divine Life, the world is also conformed to its Redeemer in whom the grace of union elevates the Sacred Humanity to such a degree of union that it subsists in the Divine Person of the Word.

One can understand, then, that the world can find no salvation unless it lives by a grace of union with God, a grace which is immeasurably below the grace of the hypostatic union but which nevertheless resembles that ineffable union and derives from it, just as the Christian's adoptive sonship resembles the Divine Sonship from which it is derived.

First and foremost, Holy Orders is a power of sanctifying and of unifying in the unity of Divine Life. For this reason it contains the necessary elements for the world of sanctification—the power to remit sin and the power to bring souls to supernatural birth.

It may be objected that the latter is not a specifically priestly power since Baptism may be validly conferred by a lay person. But this would be to ignore the exigencies of supernatural life which, like all forms of life, has an innate tendency to grow and develop to full maturity.

The life of grace, even when it has begun by the administration of Baptism by a lay person, cannot attain its due perfection without remaining in close dependence on the sacrament of Holy Orders. It needs the priest to forgive sin and to consecrate the Eucharist and to give the last anointing; it needs the bishop to confer Confirmation, the sacrament of maturity.

Power to sanctify, power to unite the life of man to the life of God, power to reach into the deep recesses of our being and to transform us by the initial gift and by the subsequent development of adoptive sonship of God—all this is contained in the sacrament of Holy Orders. The power of Holy Orders transforms our mode of being; it must also transform our mode of acting.

As a sacrament whose function is to achieve unity, Holy Orders must bring unity into our life of action by bringing the whole range of human activity into conformity with the divine action, thereby establishing unity between human action and the sanctity of God. The active life of man must be geared to the Divine Life planted in his soul through sanctifying grace.

We must act in a manner that is true to our nature, true to our super-nature as sons of God. Made like unto God by the gift of grace, we must act in a Godlike manner. Holy Orders effects union between human and divine action in the first instance by implanting in the soul the unifying principle of Divine Life, and then by intensifying that life through the other sacraments.

Are not the virtues of faith, hope and charity and the moral virtues infused into the soul with grace? Do these virtues not receive further increase when grace itself is increased by the fruitful reception of the other sacraments?

The priesthood, it is clear, by causing the Divine Life of grace to spring up in souls, implants in them an ontological principle of sanctity and unity and in doing this it also implants the principles that will issue in unity of action. These principles must indeed issue in appropriate action, in virtuous action.

When this point has been reached the sacramental rôle of the priest is terminated. But the other powers of the priest, those powers which are, as it were, grafted on his priesthood, (for example his participation in the teaching mission of the Church and in the guiding office of the Good Shepherd), the powers which a priest possesses as a member of the hierarchy, have still a large part to play in perfecting the work of unity that was begun in the depths of the human personality by the initial gift of grace.

2. *Unity of thought.*

Christ is the Truth. When human reason tries to build a system of knowledge without taking account of the one Truth which is the keystone of all knowledge, it is doomed to failure. Truth is one, and those only who accept the message of truth which Christ taught can attain that wisdom which reconciles all values, the lowest with the highest, *jungens ima summis.*

Faith in the divine truth is at once the guarantee and the first-fruits of the perfect unity of those intelligences which walk in the light towards the fullness of light. In this domain, too, Holy Orders must fulfil its function of achieving unity; it must be a storehouse of light and truth, it must continue the rôle of Christ Who is ever accessible to the minds that seek Him.

The mission to teach which the Lord confided to the Apostles and to their successors, the bishops, is one of the prerogatives of the hierarchy since the gift of infallibility has been conferred on the unanimous teaching of the bishops.

The teaching ministry of the priesthood constitutes a bond of union between Christ and human minds. When the Church teaches she does not invent anything. This is a sure guarantee for the faithful; they are not asked to believe the teaching of this or that doctor or bishop or pope, but to believe divine truth only.

Faith in the truths preached by the Church puts us in direct contact with Christ. It is Christ Who speaks, Christ Who is the centre of all revealed truth, Christ Who illumines our intelligences from within. The Truth proposed and the voice that teaches and the light that inspires faith are all one since they all centre upon the one Person of the Redeemer.

This unity of thought in the vast multitudes of the faithful (the *ecclesia discens*), is in itself a miracle of harmony. The miracle does not consist solely in the fact that all believe the same truth, but especially in the fact that all believe that truth *freely*.

Faith is essentially a free act. One cannot draw near the Saviour without sharing in the beatitude promised in the words "the truth will set you free". To make an act of faith is not simply to free the reason from prejudice and error; it is to make an act of personal adherence because one wishes and chooses to do so.

The close harmony existing in the body of the Christian people, a harmony centred and based on Christ the One Master and the Unique source of Life, is not something static; it is the harmony of a living unity in which each member of the Body contributes his personal share.

All Christians believe the same truth and for the same motive, but each one believes in his own way. No two acts of faith have the same intensity, just as no two acts of charity have the same degree of love.

We are far indeed from the abdication of personality which rationalist thinkers of all ages have denounced as the attitude of soul of the believer. Among us, on the contrary, there is full scope for free initiative because the adherence of each member to Christ is *free* and *wholehearted* and Jesus Christ is all in all to us. He is the Voice that speaks and the Message that is spoken. Jesus Christ alone can build a work of perfect unity which is at the same time a work of perfect liberty.

Unity of thought; unity that is freely accepted; harmony of heart among people whose search for truth has ended in the welcoming light of Christ—such is the achievement of Holy Orders. It is a source of true thinking, just as it is the sacrament of supernatural fecundity. But it must also be the principle of true loving: for attached to the power of Orders is that of jurisdiction.

3. *Unity of Will.*

On the surface nothing seems more remote from love than the power of establishing and maintaining legal order, *potestas moraliter alios obligandi*—the power of obliging others to right conduct. In its legislative, judicial and corrective aspects, the exercise of jurisdiction seems foreign to the character of the shepherd who goes in search of his straying sheep and leads them back to the paternal fold.

But it is none the less true that the power of jurisdiction exists for the purpose of uniting the hearts of the faithful and helping them to grow in love.

It is erroneous to conceive ecclesiastical jurisdiction as an end in itself. If at times in the history of the Church the exercise of juridical authority has taken on the guise of strength divorced from love, this has been the result of an abuse of the power itself. Since it was instituted to lead souls in the way of salvation, all ecclesiastical jurisdiction exists for the salvation of souls through charity.

Is there a single law of the Church which does not promote charity? When the constitutions of Religious Orders regulate the details of daily life they are simply defining a special way of loving God and one's neighbour.

Even when the Church tries cases in ecclesiastical tribunals, even when she pronounces judgment and inflicts penalties, we can still hear an echo of the Master's voice saying, "every branch that beareth fruit he will purge it . . . if anyone abide not in me he shall be cast forth as a branch and shall wither and they shall gather him up and cast him into the fire and he burneth[8].

---

[8] John, XV, 6.

If the second half of the text quoted refers to the definite penalty of hell-fire, it also helps to explain a certain aspect of ecclesiastical jurisdiction here below when the Church excludes unworthy members from the community of the faithful.

Charity towards the whole Body sometimes requires the amputation or cauterization of diseased parts. Since the Church is charged with the care of the whole Body, she is occasionally forced to exercise charity towards the whole at the expense of the part.

We should add, however, that ecclesiastical punishment can also turn to the good of the guilty party since chastisement here below can lead to a sincere spirit of repentance and a renewal of heart.

Hence it is clear that in the exercise of punitive justice, as in the domain of legislation, the Church is primarily concerned with the growth of the whole Body in unity and love. It is in this sense alone that her pastoral rôle can be understood.

The Good Shepherd in His own life on earth has left us a well-defined picture of true pastoral activity. It is a service of love and its purpose is to bring souls to live by love.

How far that love-service can go was shown by the Good Shepherd Himself when He laid down His life for His flock. For them He exposed Himself to danger. He delivered Himself up for their salvation. He gave Himself completely for the flock so that they might live in love. He has described the loving unity He came to establish by drawing a picture of the scattered sheep being gathered into a single fold: *Fiet unum ovile et unus pastor*[9].

Charity alone gathers the flock of Christ into the same fold because charity alone can inspire joyous and free obedience to the one Shepherd; charity makes the flock feed in peace in the same pasture; charity makes them live the same life.

Charity is the bond of union that unites all wills, inspiring them to accept the conditions of life in the one fold. The law of charity guides the flock in all its ways: *cognosco meas et cognoscunt me meae*[10].

Since Christ has so clearly defined the pastoral office, there is no room for any other authoritative interpretation of it. Peter and the eleven, the Pope and the bishops—in a word, the organized

[9] John, X, 16.
[10] John, X, 14.

hierarchy of the Church—are enlisted in the service of love. Church administration, like the priesthood itself, is a ministry of love.

Holy Orders, sacrament of Christian unity, introduces us to a new participation in the life of the Trinity. The unity in question is not the unity of a material aggregate, but the organic unity of a living being. The life of the Church, like the life of every living thing, is characterized by a hierarchial order between the various living cells which co-operate in the development of life.

The sacred ministry has always included and always will include a hierarchy. With jealous care, the Church has obstinately defended the Christian hierarchy against all those who tried to abolish it on the pretext of thereby achieving greater uniformity in the Church.

Ignatius of Antioch speaks with deep feeling of the vital harmony that exists between the members of the Church:

"Let all likewise respect the deacons as Christ Himself, and the bishop as the image of the Father. As regards the priests, they are, so to speak, God's senate and His council. Without this hierarchy, one cannot speak of a Church"[11].

The priesthood is hierarchically constituted in the image of the eternal hierarchy existing in God, a hierarchy as real as the Divine Persons Who form it.

When we speak of a hierarchy in God we do not mean that there is any subordination of Persons in the Trinity; but we refer to the order of the divine processions, a hierarchy of relations according to which life, light and love originate eternally in the Father Who communicates them to the Son by way of generation, and Who with the Son communicates the same Divine Life and light and love to the Holy Ghost.

This divine hierarchy is the eternal prototype of perfect unity of life, for there is no unity in God except that by which Father, Son and Holy Ghost are from all eternity one and the same God. Here we touch the heart of the mystery.

In God there is not first of all a divine unity from which springs a trinity of Persons; nor is there a trinity of Persons who unite to form a single Divine Nature; but from all eternity there exists one

---

[11] *Ad Trallianos,* 3; P.G., V, 677.
[12] Matthew, XXVIII, 18.

God Who is one only God by being eternally a hierarchy of Persons and who is a Trinity of Persons, only by being the one God.

In the unity of the divine hierarchy there is an eternal surge of Divine Life and light and love from the Father to the Son and from the Father and the Son to the Holy Ghost. Thanks to this order of intra-Trinitarian life revealed by God, unity in its divine principle and perfect term is not a cold impersonal thing. It is wisdom and love ever surging into life, ever welling forth, inexhaustible.

In the sacrament of Holy Orders we can see an expression (immanent on earth by grace) of the divine hierarchy. The priesthood truly expresses an aspect of the Life of the Father, Son and Holy Ghost. To appreciate this truth, we must examine the sacrament of Holy Orders in relation to the eternal priesthood of Christ on which it is founded.

Every priest shares in the ministry and in the power of the great High-Priest, Jesus Christ, and like Him he is charged with revealing to souls the secret resources of Trinitarian Life that are contained in the power of Holy Orders. When the Son said *"Data est mihi omnis potestas in coelo et in terra—*All power is given me in heaven and on earth"—He was speaking of His power to reestablish all things in Himself. Whence did He receive that power?

It came to Him as part of His eternal Sonship in the bosom of the Father. As Son, He is the term of the divine fecundity of the Father. That divine fruitfulness was to overflow from the Son on all souls who would believe in Him; the temporal mission of the Son on earth is an extension of His eternal generation from the Father.

The priesthood of Christ, then, is primarily an expression of the divine prerogative which He possesses as Son, the prerogative of disposing of all the riches of the Father. Life and light and love can be born of the Son on earth because He possesses them eternally in Heaven, because with Him they are eternally born of the Father.

A priest in whom the priesthood of Christ is prolonged, is a distributor of the same divine riches—Life, light and love—which issue from the Father. Like the Son, a priest is a permanent source of divine gifts. His powers of regenerating souls, of forgiving sin, of enlightening minds and nourishing hearts, know no decrease and can never be exhausted.

At any hour of the day or night, at any time of life, no matter how great his personal faults, a priest bears in himself the power of renewing Divine Life. He is a father in whom souls recognize a power that is more than human, a power that is not of this world. Even when he betrays his calling, Christians respect in him the seal with which the Father has sealed him for all eternity.

A priest participates in the riches of the Father,through the Son and in union with the Son. What exactly does this mean? We have seen that the priestly ministry consists in the generation of adoptive sons of God and from this point of view it would seem that the priestly office is solely a share in the fecundity of the Father. The Father is Life in its source, and a priest is a minister of this Source of Divine Life.

But there is another office which the priest alone can fulfil—the offering of sacrifice. Let us look a little closer at this ministry of mediation which is found in all religions, even in those which do not include any idea of spiritual regeneration.

Every religion has its altars before which stands a priest charged with offering a sacrifice, or as the Epistle to the Hebrews puts it, *ut offerat dona pro peccatis.*[13] A priest is charged with the office of reconciliation through the offering of sacrifice, and in the Church of Christ this is the first and most essential duty of those who have been ordained with the imposition of hands—*cum impositione manuum presbyterii* [14].

Since the Father is the Source of all life, everything must be offered up to the Father so that it may receive life; and since everything has suffered disorder through the sin of man, so everything must be reconciled to the Father.

Sacrifice is the total oblation of everything without reservation. Only one Person can make such a total oblation because He alone has taken all things to Himself and has raised all things up in the offering of Himself.

The Son of God alone, Who by His Incarnation became the centre of all things and Who brought everything on earth into union with His existence as God Incarnate—the Son alone sanctifies everything by offering everything in union with the oblation He made of Himself.

This act of Christ was performed once but it remains forever:

---

[13] Hebrews., V, 1.
[14] I Tim., IV, 14.

It was a unique offering whose efficacy does not require that it be made a second or third time. But the offering must abide, even when Christ is taken down from the Cross, even when the Cross is taken from Calvary.

The offering He made must continue so that the reconciliation of mankind may be completed. That is the reason why the Catholic priest continues to offer sacrifice.

What does he offer? What did the Son of God offer? The Son of God offered Himself and He offered all creation in union with Himself.

The priest offers the Son and the whole universe with the Son; or with greater truth we must say that the Son offers Himself in His priest. For the Son still needs arms that will rise to Heaven in a gesture of supplication; He needs a voice to utter the words "This is My Body . . . This is My Blood". He needs hands to hold the chalice and to break the bread. He needs knees to bend to the earth. The arms, the hands, the voice, the knees—they are the priest.

There is a mysterious identification of the priest with Christ. And since the offering he makes includes the elevation of all things to the Father, the priest like the Son is a mediator between God and man—*mediator Dei et hominum* [15].

By his office he is another son, the *alter ego* of the Only Begotten of the Father, Who alone holds the secrets of birth and rebirth— *Omnia per ipsum facta sunt* [16]. *Per eum reconciliare omnia in ipsum* [17].

No wonder, then, that the priestly ministry extends to everything on earth. The priest blesses bread and water and the fields and the harvest and beasts and men. He has offered them all to the Father in union with the Son and now he returns to them bringing them the Blessing of the Father.

After the hour of sacrifice comes the hour of the resurrection. The world, offered up in sacrifice, recovers its pristine purity and the holiness of its primordial tendency towards God. It can sing again the Magnificat of its new ascension to the Father. When the priest raises his hand in blessing he is the minister of the Son

---

[15] I Tim., II, 5.
[16] John, I, 3.
[17] Coloss., I, 3.

Who sacrificed Himself and Who is now in the bosom of the Father.

The priesthood, then, establishes a close degree of conformity between the priest and the Son of God. It is also in a special way a sacrament of the Holy Ghost. Since Holy Orders is the sacrament of unity it must be principally the work of the Holy Ghost Who is the universal Spirit of union and Who in the Trinity is the personal subsistent bond of union between the Father and Son.

By his temporal mission, too, it is the Holy Ghost Who unites the world to the Father and the Son, and Who gives the Father and the Son to the world. No degree of harmony or sanctity or loving union is possible except by the power of the Spirit.

How does the Holy Spirit exercise His function as Spirit of union in the sacrament of Orders to such a degree that He becomes, as it were, the soul of the priesthood? We must also examine how the fecundity of the Father, distributed on earth by the Son, is prolonged among us by the Holy Spirit.

To appreciate this mystery, we must begin by accepting the conditions that govern supernatural life as already indicated in Chapter I, where we defined the effects of the sacraments. Supernatural life does not consist merely in living by the Father and the Son, but in living in conformity to the Father and Son. Without conformity there can be no life of union with God.

The life of the Father and the Son is a mutual giving of each to the other so that together they become the origin whence proceeds the Holy Ghost in Whom they abide as the term of their union. This eternal mutual donation of Persons is the whole Life of the Blessed Trinity.

It follows that if man is to participate in the life of the Father and of the Son he must also abide in the Holy Ghost. This is the reason why no one can be justified except in the Holy Ghost.

The priest who is called to share in the mission of the Son by radiating the life that comes from the Father must necessarily receive the gift of the Holy Ghost. To reject this conclusion would be to involve oneself in contradiction; it would imply that the priest gives a life that does not vivify.

It is for this reason that the Holy Ghost abides in the priesthood and that He is given to souls in every sacrament administered by a priest.

He is given in Baptism when supernatural life commences; He is given in Penance when the sinner is reborn to the life he has lost; He is given in Matrimony and in all the sacraments since each one of them signifies and produces Divine Life or an increase of that Life.

Holy Orders is the source of all sacramental life and hence it is a rich fountainhead of the gifts of the Holy Ghost. When a priest is ordained by the imposition of hands, he receives the Holy Ghost; when he receives the power to forgive sin, he needs a further infusion of the Spirit: *Accipe Spiritum Sanctum; quorum remiseris peccata remittuntur eis*[18].

The gift of the Holy Ghost forms an integral part of the sanctifying ministry of the priest, which is, of course, the most important function of the priesthood. Does the Holy Ghost fill an equally important rôle in the priest's ministry as a teacher and guide of souls?

This question will not cause any difficulty if one considers Divine Life in its full reality. Divine Life is not separable or even distinct from light and love. The life of God is light; it is also love. The same conditions which govern the origin of life also apply to the origin of light and love.

If the Holy Ghost Who is given to souls in the sacraments becomes through His mission as Sanctifier the connatural element, as it were, in which Divine Life is born and comes to full development, He must at the same time be an inexhaustible fount of light and love.

This is understandable because there is only one way to abide in the light and that is to abide close to the very source of truth. The Father is that Source; the Son has received the mission to open Its treasures to souls; the Holy Ghost keeps us in close union with It. It is in the Holy Ghost and only in the Holy Ghost that we can drink from the fountains of the Saviour that spring from the depths of the Father.

This is why Our Lord promised to send the Apostles and their successors the " Spirit of truth ", the Spirit of that Truth which was Jesus Christ in Person—*Ego sum veritas*[19], the Spirit of truth

---

[18] *Rituale Romanum.*
[19] John, XIV, 6.

Who gives understanding by bringing human minds into union with eternal truth. He is the Spirit who bestows infallibility both on the teaching of that truth and on the faith of Christians.

The indestructible harmony existing in the Church between the pastors who preach the truth and the flock who believe the truth is possible only in and through the Holy Ghost.

The same must be said for what regards the conduct of the people of God. There is only one way to avoid going astray, namely, to follow close in the steps of the Saviour. The Shepherd who goes before the flock, He is also, as He told us, the Way, the only path that leads to the Father. We are sure of progressing in the right direction if we keep to the right road, if we place our feet in the tracks of Him Who is appointed to lead us.

Who but the Holy Ghost can keep us united to the Saviour? It is the Holy Ghost alone Who guarantees that we follow straight in the footsteps of the guiding Shepherd, Who has also become the Way by which we travel to the Father.

It follows that ecclesiastical jurisdiction, in its function of guiding, strengthening and correcting the conduct of the members of Christ, is exercised in the Holy Ghost, since it is essentially an exercise of love: *finis autem praecepti est charitas*[20].

Life, light, love—they come to us and divinize us from the Father, through the Son and in the Holy Ghost. The function of the priesthood is to make this Divine Life, light and love spring up here on earth.

We have already cited the ardent words in which St. Ignatius exhorted the Christians to charity. When he wished to teach them respect for the hierarchy, which is, so to speak, the skeletal structure of the Mystical Body, he pointed out that in each of the three major Orders there is an image of one of the Divine Persons.

In the bishop he sees the Father, in the deacon the Son, while he calls the priests God's council and senate[21]. Without dwelling on the comparisons suggested by the holy bishop—he uses them as symbols and illustrations—we think it interesting to note that St. Ignatius regarded the ecclesiastical hierarchy as an image and a manifestation of the hierarchy existing in the Blessed Trinity.

In this he expresses the living faith of the early centuries which

---

[20] I Tim., I, 5.
[21] Op. cit., et Ad Magnes., VI, 1; P.G., V, 668 where the priests are compared with the Apostles.

saw the presence of the Blessed Trinity figured in every Christian activity. Just as all Christian activity was subject to the guidance of the pastors of the Church, so, too, it was under the constant influence of the Trinity.

In the preceding chapters we have tried to justify this attitude of faith by showing that Holy Orders is the sacrament that is specially designed to bring the world under the influence of the Life of the Three Divine Persons. The ecclesiastical hierarchy is more than a mere symbol of the divine hierarchy; it is a permanent and ever active participation in the life of the hierarchy of Three Persons in God.

Rather than regard the bishops, deacons and priests as personifications of the Father and the Son, we prefer to regard the functions of the priesthood in its various degrees as the gift of the whole Trinity with a view to the generation, instruction and guidance of Christians in their supernatural life.

In doing this, Holy Orders displays its special power of establishing harmony between Heaven and earth. Here, too, appears the rich meaning of the priestly character. Is there any wonder that Holy Orders should confer a character since, as we have seen, the sacramental character consists in a spiritual and indelible power of exercising a public function in the Church? A priest is by definition a minister of the merciful power of God.

As regards the sacerdotal character, there is free discussion among theologians as to whether the episcopal character is distinct from the priestly character, or whether the episcopate is an extension and a complement of the priesthood. Perhaps the practice followed in ordination ceremonies will help us to choose a solution.

The Church strongly upholds the distinction between the various grades in the hierarchy and teaches as a dogma that bishops are superior to priests [22]. But she does not consecrate any man a bishop unless he is already a priest. In doing this she asserts that there is a necessary continuity between the priesthood and the episcopate, and she seems to regard the latter as the full development of the order conferred in the priesthood.

To understand this, we must remember that here, as in all the sacraments, we are dealing with Life, Divine Life. Now life is always characterized by continuity. A tree first produces flowers

---

[22] *Conc. Trid., Sess.* XXIII, cap. 7; Denz. 967.

and later fruit. But it is the same life, the same vital force, which produces both and which will not yield fruit until it has first blossomed into flower.

This may help us to understand the various degrees in the hierarchy. They are inseparable though distinct, both in their substance and in their powers. In this respect, too, Holy Orders is seen as a participation in the Life of the Trinity, since it includes the mystery of distinction in unity, and hierarchy in community, a phenomenon that characterizes all life, both in time and eternity.

To conclude:

Christian Marriage emphasizes by a kind of paradox, the necessity for the sacrament of Holy Orders in the supernatural destiny of man. Here is the paradox: Matrimony, which like every other sacrament produces grace, and which assimilates the life of husband and wife to the life of the Divine Persons, exists primarily for the procreation of children. Its primary end is to permit man and woman, wedded in Christ, to perform those acts which of themselves are apt for the generation of children. What kind of children? Christian children?

Unfortunately, no. Whether parents be legitimately married in Church or not, the children of their union are born pagans. neither the virtue of the parents nor the sanctity of the sacrament of Matrimony nor even the heroic sanctity of husband and wife can change that fact. Their child is born deprived of original justice and turned away from God.

Matrimony needs the sacrament of Holy Orders as its necessary complement. Granted that a child may be validly baptized by a lay person, the fact remains that the Supernatural Life thus received in Baptism needs the ministry of a priest if It is to survive and develop.

Without Penance and Confirmation and the Eucharist what would become of our Divine Life? We can understand, then, that Holy Orders and Matrimony, though in different ways, are sacraments that are instituted for the good of the many. Both have to deal with generation. While Matrimony unites the partners with a view to carnal generation, Holy Orders gives the priest the power of supernatural fecundity.

Here is the essential distinction between the two sacraments.

Husband and wife, two persons, become one flesh and together form a single principle of life, whereas the priest by remaining alone in his celibacy radiates and communicates the fecundity of the Father on earth.

Hence it comes that the sacraments of Matrimony and Holy Orders while presenting distinct and contrary characteristics, nevertheless complement each other. Marriage has a limited end. The generation and education of children, even of numerous children, remains a function of the smallest social unit—the family.

Holy Orders, on the contrary, is a function of the whole universe. A priest owes himself and gives himself to the whole world. His spiritual fecundity is never exhausted because it derives from the Holy Ghost.

Opposites, like body and soul, Matrimony and Holy Orders are necessary to each other; they are parts of the same whole. The generation of children of God and members of Christ would be impossible if marriage did not ensure the continuity of the human race, that race which since the Incarnation has become the race of the Saviour Himself.

On the other hand, the carnal generation of children would lack all supernatural and Christian value if there were no further generation and regeneration of souls by the Holy Ghost.

The whole Christian order depends on maintaining close unity between the natural and the supernatural. It is Christ Who harmonizes the order of the flesh and of the spirit because to each He has given the power not only to signify but to enter into vital union with the Father and the Son and the Holy Ghost.

CHAPTER VIII

EXTREME UNCTION

To UNDERSTAND the meaning and scope of the sacrament of Extreme Unction we must first consider the practice of the Church in the administration of this sacrament. What the Church does in practice is always a special manifestation of a dogmatic truth. As regards Extreme Unction we must dismiss the idea sometimes expressed that it is the " sacrament of the sick ".

A person may be laid up in bed with a fairly high temperature, but that does not of itself qualify him for the reception of the sacrament; not, for example, if the temperature is caused by a mild dose of influenza. On the other hand, Extreme Unction is not simply the sacrament of those who are about to die. A condemned man awaiting execution cannot be anointed even though death is imminent and inevitable.

But if an accident victim lies dying in the street every effort is made to give him the last sacrament, presuming that he is baptized and properly disposed. This leads us to the definition of Extreme Unction as the sacrament of those who are ill and in danger of death.

It is important to keep this elementary notion in mind if we are to appreciate the special rôle of this sacrament which comes to strengthen man's weakness on the threshold of death. Extreme Unction, in fact, produces a double series of effects; one set of effects supposes illness, the other supposes that death is near. To which of these effects shall we give priority? The question is not without importance.

There is general agreement among theologians that the grace of the last anointing produces three effects: it gives strength to overcome the difficulties that assail a Christian at the hour of death; it remits sin and the temporal punishment due to sin; finally, it causes the recovery of health if this is profitable for the soul.

Before the Council of Trent there was some degree of hesitation in defining the principal effect of Extreme Unction. Dun Scotus, exaggerating the position of St. Bonaventure, thought that the remission of venial sin was the most important contribution that Extreme Unction had to make in preparing man for the Beatific Vision[1].

At first sight, this theory seems to have an advantage over all others. There cannot be question of positing the remission of mortal sin as the principal end of the sacrament. It is a sacrament of the living, and Bellarmine later stressed the fact that it does not remit mortal sin, except in the case where such sin has not been remitted by the sacrament of Penance[2].

Neither can the restoration of bodily health be the principal purpose of the sacrament. In the tradition of the Church, this effect has always been regarded as conditional ("if bodily health is profitable to the soul ") and it is impossible for the primary effect of a sacrament to be merely conditional.

In defining the scope of this sacramental means of sanctification, we must look for something that is always effected when the sacrament is validly administered and fruitfully received. This thesis would seem to be incontrovertible. It was the point of view taken by St. Thomas, and it differs greatly from the more common theological opinion on the subject since the Council of Trent.

According to the Angelic Doctor, Extreme Unction first of all produces a positive spiritual effect, namely, a grace of strength to resist the temptations and the lethargy that threaten man in his last agony. At the same time, and while producing this first effect, the sacrament also alleviates the burden which illness lays on the soul of the dying person. The word " *alleviabit* " in the Epistle of St. James is thus given an objective and spiritual significance[3].

Finally since these are the effects of grace and since grace is incompatible with the existence of sin in the soul, that very same grace remits mortal and venial sin, provided that the soul does not offer any obstacle[4].

The Council of Trent did not " canonize " any of these theological interpretations, but the text of the Council helps us to choose between them. It states that Extreme Unction surrounds the

---

[1] *In IV Sent.*, dist. XXIII.
[2] Op. omnia, t. III, *De Extrema Unctione*, c. VIII, pp. 759-760.
[3] James, V. 15.
[4] *Supplem.*, q. 30, a. 1. c.

last moments of life with a strong bastion of defence, *finem vitae tanquam firmissimo quodam praesidio munivit*[5].

Again, in defining this sacrament of the Christian's last agony, the Council uses an expression that condenses a whole section of dogmatic teaching in a few words: it is the sacrament that *consummates* Christian life—*consummativim vitae Christianae*[6].

The final crowning of life does not consist simply in the forgiveness of sin and the remission of temporal punishment due to sin. These are merely negative effects, necessary indeed as negative conditions for the flowering of supernatural life. But one does not fully describe the sun by saying that it is "the conqueror of darkness"; the expression leaves out of account the radiant power of the sun which yields light and heat and which promotes life.

Similarly, in speaking of the sacrament of Extreme Unction, we must concentrate on its positive effects. Through the dark struggle of a soul at grips with death, we must see the reception of the last sacrament as an offering of self that goes to the extreme limit of self-oblation, as a gift of God that closes the last chapter of life, rousing, strengthening and guiding the soul home to the Father.

To understand the full import of the last anointing, we must follow the spirit of the definitions of the Council of Trent and try to probe this mystery of a life that reaches ultimate fulfilment in death.

Death gives to life its final orientation. Even pagans recognise the unique significance of death when they build memorials to their dead, to their warriors killed in battle, and to many an unknown hero. Why, we may ask, do they not raise statues to the living? The reason is that the living, unfortunately, may yet fall back and undo by a single stroke all that their courage has achieved over many years.

We have known heroes of the 1914-1918 war, men decorated for their services, who failed in the Second World War and who were justly condemned to death. Their lives, instead of growing in heroism to the very end, were spoiled by a series of crimes that culminated in treason.

On the other hand, a man who dies a hero sets a final seal on the value of his life. Neither his background, nor his personal

---

[5] *Sess.* XIV, c. 9; Denz. 907.
[6] ibid.

status, nothing, in a word, can change one syllable of the epitaph he has written in his own sweat and blood.

Death possesses the formidable power of setting an indelible seal on the value of life. For this reason, a man who is about to die takes his whole life in his hands, so to speak, and offers it up in a final gesture of consecration. Such as he is in his acceptance of death, such will be forever the meaning of his earthly existence.

Death writes *"finis"* to the story of life, but for a person who knows that there is life beyond the grave, death means something much more profound; it fixes a person immutably in relation to the life beyond. At the moment of death, a moment which no previous act of man can determine—even though all his previous acts bear weight in his final decision—man must offer himself to God in an act of supreme and all-embracing self-oblation.

When a man is in his agony his last offering takes on the aspect of a deeply moving drama from the fact that he makes his supreme offering at the moment when his earthly life is in the throes of final disintegration.

A mighty issue is at stake in the last moments of life. There is a whole eternity in the balance, and man has to decide that eternity in this moment of greatest weakness, when he is on the brink of the ultimate dissolution of bodily life. Does not this give us an indication of the primary end of the sacrament of Extreme Unction?

Undoubtedly, the sacrament remits sin and temporal punishment as part of God's merciful plan to prepare the dying person for the Beatific Vision. But above and beyond this what is needed is that man in his utter weakness should receive the strength he needs to make the most decisive and at times the most difficult choice of all—the decision to die as a Christian.

It is normal, then, that the most common opinion of theologians is that *gratia roborans,* the grace of strength, is the primary effect of Extreme Unction. Well before the Council of Trent, St. Thomas had decided in favour of this view. There is an art of dying just as there is an art of living, and for a Christian there is only one way to die, namely, to die like Christ.

Christ died. He suffered the death agony. In His incarnate self He made the supreme oblation of His life in the death-throes of His

Sacred Humanity when His body and soul, were being wrenched asunder. Christ offered Himself—*seipsum obtulit*.

What was the content of His oblation? In it the infinity of His personal love consecrated the whole ensemble of His earthly life, and in a single act of oblation He offered the Father all His efforts as Redeemer, all that His love had inspired Him to undertake on earth.

But Christ offered more than His efforts and His love: He offered everything with which He had come in contact; the world and all that is in it; the earth in which His human life had taken root, the elements that had sustained and nourished His human life; the air He breathed, the light that shone in His eyes. The whole universe and every creature, all were united with the dying Christ, and all were redeemed by His death.

Offering Himself as Redeemer, He also offered up the redeemed world and at the moment when His mortal nature was dissolved He offered all things to the Father so that the grace of His Resurrection would descend on the whole world.

Dying thus, Christ willed that we should ever remember the Cross, the symbol of His death-struggle, and that His death cry should reach us re-echoing through the centuries. Our Saviour Who has gone before us through the portals of death did not hesitate to let fall that cry of woe which expressed the full reality of His suffering and the full reality of His human nature: "My God, my God, why hast thou thou forsaken me?"

In the depth of His human weakness He planted the full strength of God so that all those who like Him must pass through the agony of death might receive through His death the grace to sustain the burden of their oblation to the very end. For the Christian must offer himself with Christ in the total self-oblation of death.

Sometimes one may feel inclined to ask why Christ, the second Adam Who restored us to the divine friendship, did not also give us back the gift of immortality. Some people believe that the Saviour's sacrifice would have been more sublime if by His death He had wiped out the debt of death for all those who would enter into union with Him.

But even though we regard death as a decree of God's avenging justice, it remains a disposition of His loving providence and the reason for it is enshrined in the mystery of the death of Our Redeemer. Our supreme good, our most heroic and grandiose destiny is to be able to offer ourselves in total oblation as Christ offered Himself on the Cross.

We need not seek to know how the first Adam, endowed with the gift of immortality, would have made his act of total self-oblation if he had remained faithful to God. We cannot doubt that even in a painless existence Adam would still have been obliged to make an act of total oblation.

For our part, let us limit ourselves to considering in the light of Christ's death all the richness of the offering by which we are privileged to consummate our present life by a supreme act of conformity with the Son of God.

Behold how in the weakness of a defectible nature and in the dark stream of death a current of life asserts itself, a current which has been growing in strength through all the vicissitudes of life, a current which at the end carries us forward into the ocean of divine light.

A dying person offers himself in the image of Christ's death. He offers his whole personality, his personal life with its checkered pattern of triumph and failure, his progress and his repeated backsliding, everything that forms an integral part of his personal existence.

Life is sometimes said to be a series of recommencements. At the moment of death, life receives its final fixation and is stamped forever with that definitive permanence that marks all things that die.

A dying person offers more than himself. He offers everything that was in any way connected with his personal life. He is a thing of earth, the roots of his life are deep in the earth which nourished him and raised him to manhood.

In his turn, he enriched the world to a greater or lesser degree with the gifts of his personality. In his final act of oblation, a dying man offers all that was, as it were, the extension of his life on earth through the impact of his personality on the world.

The Christian must, then, die as Christ died. He must resemble Christ in his death to self so that in him the power of Christ's death may triumph. Extreme Unction is the sacrament which contains the secret of this active conformity to Christ in the final consummation of His sacrifice.

Let us repeat: the Christian's conformity with Christ must be achieved by the offering of himself at the moment of his final weakness. Extreme Unction is not the sacrament of all those who are about to die; it is administered only to those who are ill and in danger of death.

For Christ Himself died in weakness and His sacrifice derived greater value from the fact that He made His total offering precisely in a state of extreme weakness. He accepted that final weakness so that the glory of His risen life might dawn through the eclipse of His mortal life.

All who wish to die in Christ so as to rise again with Him must share in the weakness of the agonizing Saviour. Death, in fact, is not only a preparation for the vision of God; it is also a preparation for the resurrection of the body.

O profound mystery! In one single act of self-oblation, the exultant surge of a life that triumphs is united to the last breath of a life that dies. Each in his own death united to Christ renews in himself what the dying Christ did for all. At death, the Christian participates in the sacrifice of Calvary and makes his own those words which announce the salvation of the world: *consummatum est.*

Precisely because Extreme Unction is the sacrament of those who are ill and in danger of death, it is not easy to see in what way it includes a participation in the mystery of the Blessed Trinity.

Admittedly as part of the scheme of redemption, Extreme Unction concerns each of the Three Divine Persons—the Father Who sent His Son to save the world, the Son Who offered the redeeming sacrifice, and the Holy Ghost Who unites the redeemed to Christ as the members of a body are united with the head.

Extreme Unction is a part of the whole economy of God's mercy in our regard in which the Three Persons are always divinely active. The last anointing marks the final stage of a life which began at Baptism and which never ceased to be a participation in the life of the Three Persons Who are one God.

Can we detect any further relation, any special point of contact between the weakness of a dying person and the omnipotence of the Trinity? There is indeed complete contrast between the two, and only the infinite and all-merciful love of God can harmonize the contrasts in the unity of reciprocal love.

In spite of the superficial and obvious contrast, we believe that in the depths of this mystery of death there is an echo of the personal relations within the Blessed Trinity. Christ offering Himself on the Cross performed a strictly personal act. What we call the drama of Calvary would not have had infinite value if it had not been the infinite offering made by a Divine Person, God, the Second Person of the Trinity.

A dying person must conform himself to the Person of the Word, the same Divine Person Whom He was called to resemble from the moment of his supernatural birth and through the various stages of his growth in grace. Our religion has no meaning if it is not the gift of one's whole personality to the Person of the God Who saved us.

But, as we have said before, where one Divine Person is active there also are the other Persons of the Trinity. Whosoever enters by grace into the life and love of the Divine Word is necessarily caught up in the surge of Divine Life that flows eternally between the Father, Son and Holy Ghost.

In treating of the mystery of the Blessed Trinity, perhaps there is not sufficient emphasis laid on the reciprocal indwelling of each Divine Person in the others. We shall return to this mystery of circuminsession when we come to treat of the Blessed Eucharist in the next chapter.

Each Divine person lives in the others, firstly by the absolute identity of the Divine Nature, but also by a personal movement of knowledge and love. The Father is in the Son by the knowledge He has of the Son and by His love of the Son; the Son is in the Father by a return of knowledge and love.

There is, then, a special way in which each Divine Person communicates Himself to the other Persons in God. What, we may ask, characterizes this divinely personal mode of communication between the Divine Persons?

First of all, since it is a personal act, it is both conscious and voluntary. But it is something more than that. It is a perfect and total offering in which each Person gives to the others the totality of the Divine Essence with which each is really identified. The Father is the whole Godhead; the Son and the Holy Ghost are the same Godhead. But Father, Son and Holy Ghost are God each with His own personal attributes.

For a mortal creature, however, the only adequate offering he can make in imitation of the total and personal self-oblation in God is the supreme offering of his life; for mortal man, that offering is achieved only by death. Man makes his most perfect self-oblation by giving himself in death.

There is a sense of the absolute inherent in the mystery of death. Not only does man, then, give his all, consciously and voluntarily, but his act of giving is irrevocable. His dying act of oblation precludes all drawing back. With his last breath, he yields himself up completely without any possibility of undoing his oblation.

These considerations shed light on the reason for the sacrifice of the Cross. It was not merely that Christ on the Cross offered all human nature united with the offering of His own Sacred Humanity; He had already made this oblation from the first moment of His conception, and had ratified it repeatedly throughout the course of His life on earth.

What distinguished His offering on the Cross was that it was an offering made in the way that characterizes the mutual gift of the Divine Persons within the Trinity, in the personal way that He, the Divine Word, gives Himself totally to the Father and the Holy Ghost from all eternity.

Christ on the Cross had to give Himself in the irrevocability of death, because death is the only way in which man can imitate the divine mode of giving—by the total and absolute gift of self.

The mystery of the Cross is more than a mystery of superabundant love. It is more than a source of courage and consolation for us mere mortals who take heart at the thought of God dying for us.

In this supreme example of God's merciful love we must see, above all else, the Son of God offering Himself to God the Father, the Word Incarnate offering Himself in His Human Nature in an act of oblation that is the prolongation on earth of the eternal donation of Himself by which the Son abides in the bosom of the Father.

In this sense one can say that the Word came on earth to die. The object of His coming was indeed to save the world, and the world could not have regained the equilibrium destroyed by sin if it had not been offered up by the Son to the eternal Father.

But His offering was the offering made by a Divine Person, and when a Divine Person offers there is no limit to His offering. God gives without measure, to the extreme limit of giving.

Since the Word assumed a mortal human nature was there not a certain congruity in the fact that He offered Himself in the only way which is absolute and definitive for a mortal, that is by dying?

The Christian who dies fortified by the sacrament of the death of Christ, conformed to the Son in death, is offered with the Son to the Father and the Holy Ghost. Let us hasten to note that the prayers of the ritual stress the fact that our Divine Life which originated in the Life of the Divine Persons receives its consummating glory in the same Blessed Trinity:

"Christian soul depart from this world in the Name of the Almighty Father Who created thee, in the Name of Jesus Christ the Son of the living God Who suffered for thee, in the Name of the Holy Ghost Who was given thee"[7].

This prayer expresses the profound mystery that envelopes the Christian at the hour of death. Conformed to the Person of the Son dying in His Sacred Humanity, the dying Christian offers himself in an act of oblation that shares in the self-oblation of the Son to the Father. Christ on the Cross left us a verbal testimony to His supreme sacrifice: "Father, into Thy hands I commend my spirit"[8].

In these words the dying Son of God gave human expression to the eternal offering by which He, the Divine Word, with the infinite power of His Divine Personality, surges towards the Father Who eternally begets Him, in a movement so divinely fruitful that mingling with the reciprocal surge of the Father's love it issues eternally in the Person of the Holy Ghost.

Perhaps we are in a better position now to understand how Extreme Unction integrates the Christian finally and forever in the life of the Blessed Trinity. He is offered to the Father in union with the Son; drawn up into the current of their mutual love, the Christian yields up his whole being with the Father and the Son in the Holy Ghost.

---

[7] *Rituale Romanum.*
[8] *Idem.*

Nor is this the whole mystery. Not only does the Father beget the Son; not only are Father and Son together the principle from which the Holy Ghost proceeds; but Father, Son and Holy Ghost abide in each other by a total donation of their Person. The mystery of God in Three Persons reaches its term in this mutual inherence of the Divine Person which is known as circuminsession.

The sacrament of Extreme Unction makes the Christian participate in this mystery of total self-oblation and mutual inherence of the Divine Persons. The dying Christian yields up his whole being; he gives himself wholly. And by grace he gives himself divinely, in the way that Person gives to Person within the Blessed Trinity. He gives himself like the Son and in union with the Son, and by this oblation his death is invested with the unique value of sharing in the inner life of the Three Persons in God.

In the death of a Christian, the Father, Son and Holy Ghost see an expression through grace and on the human level of their eternal gift of themselves, Person to Person in the identity of the same Divine Nature. Not only do the Divine Persons welcome the dying Christian in their society; by grace they effect a real conformity between man's supreme self-oblation and the divine measure of self-giving within the Trinity. This sacrament puts the final seal on the Christian's conformity with the Divine Persons.

Thanks to the last anointing, the death of a Christian takes on something of the fruitfulness of the eternal Father. By his death, he becomes a new source of grace and light and joy within the Church from which he can never more be separated.

If he dies in the Lord, we can pray to him and he can respond to our prayer. From the mystery of his death there shines a reflex of the goodness of the Father's Heart. Conformed by Extreme Unction to the Omnipotent Father, he shares in the Father's omnipotence of doing good.

His death is also bathed in the reflected glory of the Son Who is the personal image of the Father and the eternal witness of the Father's glory. When He came on earth, the Son continued to give witness to the Father, revealing in Himself the Father's goodness and sharing the divine goodness with men.

A Christian who dies in Christ is also a witness by his death. More deeply moving than the greatest eloquence, often more effective than a whole lifetime of Christian activity, a death touched by the effulgence of consummating grace is always a new revelation. Death, ancient as the history of man, is on each occasion a new experience for those who behold it.

Christian death is a final testimony to the faith, and the deathbed circumstances invest that testimony with a unique note of sincerity. One does not lie in face of death. When a Christian proclaims his unalterable attachment to God and to Christ, one realizes that his words are devoid of all the artifice of conventional rhetoric. The words of a dying man claim our belief because his final testimony shares in the testimony of the Son who testifies to what He sees[9].

Death is a manifestation of Christian faith; it is also an expression of a hope that leans on the strength of God and of a love that gives all. It is, too, a testament of peace, of that peace which the Son brought on earth: *Pax vobis.* Peace settles on the countenance, smoothing the wrinkled brow; peace joins those hands in final rest; peace enfolds the whole body that now knows no movement but the gentle ebb and flow of dying breath.

When his trembling lips speak their last vows and testify that it is sweet to die and that there is nothing more desirable than to go forward to the vision of God, the dying Christian leaves us a new revelation of the kingdom of light and joy eternal.

A Christian life offered up through its whole duration is crowned with glory in death. In death, such a life attains its final glorification and gives a new revelation of the ineffable splendour of the Son Who is the "Splendour of the Father" in the unity of the Holy Ghost.

His death also participates in the gift of the Holy Spirit, the Spirit of love, the Spirit of perfect union. His final gift of peace and union descends on the Christian deathbed. Nothing unites people so powerfully as death. Round the coffin all dissension is muted and brothers who have been at enmity find reconciliation amid their tears.

What the best efforts of parents have failed to achieve in their lifetime is brought to pass by death, whose silent grace softens even the most turbulent spirits. Death creates a bond whose strength is well expressed in the saying: "We should live in the

---

[9] John, III, 32.

spirit of our dead". The pacifying influence of a dying person is so strong that no one can escape it, except by doing violence to himself and deceiving his friends.

The dying Christian draws upon the Spirit of union and shares His power of uniting hearts. Every time that Christ leaves us in the death of one of His members, He seems to give a further fulfilment of His promise, "I will not leave you orphans"[10]. The sacrament which gives the grace to die like Him and with Him, heralds a new coming of the Spirit, the Spirit of union and concord, the Spirit of peace and consolation.

This, then, is Christian death. Strengthened by the last anointing, a Christian dies in the embrace of the Father, Son and Holy Ghost for he has reached the final stage of conformity with the Son Who at death offered Himself to the Father in the Holy Ghost.

---

[10] John, XIV, 18.

CHAPTER IX

THE BLESSED EUCHARIST

LIFE IS AN ever-welling source of enjoyment. This may appear a strange statement to make since the word "enjoyment" is commonly used in a perverted sense denoting a craze for pleasure. In reality, the word describes a perfection found in the higher living beings and it expresses their ability to relish and enjoy the good that they possess in themselves.

To live is to possess, to possess oneself and to find peace in that possession. Every animal enjoys life in this sense. Man, too, in the multiple activities of life, from the pleasures of the table to the more refined joys of art and love and intellectual pursuits, seeks contentment from the possession of the good things of life.

Supernatural life, which is life in the highest degree possible on earth, is no exception to the general law. The ultimate perfection of the supernatural life of grace consists in a certain enjoyment, the eternal enjoyment of God and of all good things in Him. Even during our earthly existence, grace offers us a foretaste of that eternal beatitude. Here and now we can enjoy God.

There is a sacrament whose principal effect consists in the enjoyment of the Godhead—it is the Blessed Eucharist. Hence we can understand the statement of St. Thomas in which he endorses the words of the pseudo-Areopagite (*Eccles. Hier., III*): the Eucharist perfects the other sacraments[1].

Whereas all the sacraments participate in the virtue that goes forth from Christ, the Eucharist contains the fullness of Christ, it contains Christ Himself. We would venture to add that while the other sacraments give life, the Blessed Eucharist gives full enjoyment of that life.

The sacrament of the Eucharist is a summit from which we can scan the whole horizon of sacramental life. That is the reason why we have reserved this sacrament to the last chapter. The end of

---

[1] S. Th., III, q. 75, a. 1, c.

life alone gives the adequate meaning of life itself. The end of supernatural life is not death, not even a death in conformity with the death of Christ; the end of the life of grace is the possession of God and the Eucharist gives a foretaste of that possession. *Et futurae gloriae nobis pignus datur.*

Let us state immediately that the following pages deal with the Eucharist as a sacrament and not as a sacrifice. If here and there we make some reference to the sacrifice of the Mass, this is done only in so far as the Mass is the indispensable condition for the existence of the sacrament. Without consecration of the Species at Mass, there is no Eucharist.

Precisely because we are considering the Eucharist as a sacrament and not as a sacrifice, it may not be easy to see the relation it bears to the Blessed Trinity. It is neither the Father nor the Holy Ghost Who becomes substantially present in the Eucharist.

The sacrament contains the body, soul and divinity of the Incarnate Son and it is the Word Incarnate Who becomes present under the Sacred Species by the act of transubstantiation. In contradistinction to the other sacraments, the Eucharist seems to be the gift of one Divine Person to the exclusion of the Father and the Holy Ghost.

In reading the Fathers, however, one is struck by the frequency with which they have recourse to the mystery of the Trinity to explain the Eucharist. There was a long controversy about the *Epiclesis,* the group of invocations addressed to the Father praying Him to send the Holy Spirit on the *oblata* so that by His power they might be transubstantiated into the Body and Blood of Christ.

The controversy was not concerned with proving the existence of such trinitarian invocations in the ancient liturgies; traces of such invocations are still to be found in the Canon of the Mass, and liturgists and Church historians, such as Hoppe, Duchesne and Cabrol, have shown that they have been in constant use in both the Eastern and Western rites since the fourth century at least.

The Epiclesis controversy centred rather on the problem whether or not the words of consecration—*Hoc est Corpus meum . . . Hic est calix sanguinis mei*—had in themselves exclusive efficacy in causing the changing of bread and wine into the Body and Blood of Christ. Since then the Church has sufficiently manifested her thought on the subject so that one must attribute the effective power of causing transubstantiation to the words of consecration alone.

This being granted, it does not follow that the mystery of the Blessed Eucharist is accomplished without the intervention of all Three Persons of the Blessed Trinity. Tradition even in the western Church points to the necessity of the intervention of the whole Trinity. In proof of this, we find certain phrases in the writings of Paschasius Radbertus where the action of the Holy Ghost is associated with the words of Christ in causing transubstantiation: *In verbo Christi per Spiritum Sanctum;* and again *virtute Spiritus Sancti per verbum Christi*[2].

In the writings of the Fathers, we not only find a clear statement of a connection between the Eucharist and the Blessed Trinity, but we can also follow an evident progression of thought in the manner in which this connection is understood. St. Justin, for example, insists on the prayer of praise and thanksgiving recited by the priest when he receives the offerings of bread and wine from the faithful, a prayer addressed to the Father in the Name of the Son and of the Holy Ghost[3].

St. Clement of Alexandria directly associates the Eucharist with the mission entrusted to the Son by the Father when He sent Him among us. The Son was given us by the Father as spiritual food to men of good will. The Church, unique as the Father, Son and Holy Ghost are unique, now gives us the Divine Word (in the Eucharist) as a mother gives milk to her children[4]. For St. Ephraim it is Christ Who takes bread and blesses it and sanctifies it in the Name of the Father and of the Holy Ghost[5].

---

[2] P.L., CXX, 1279, 1310-1312.

[3] " Deinde ei qui fratribus praeest panis offertur et poculum aquae et vini, quibus ille acceptis laudem et gloriam universorum Parenti per nomen Filii et Spiritus Sancti emittit et gratiarum actiones pro his ab illo acceptis donis prolixe exsequitur." (*Apol.* 65; *P.G.*, VI, 428).

[4] " Cum amans et benignus Pater Verbum impluisset, ipsum jam spiritale alimentum factum est bonis hominibus. O miraculum mysticum. Unus quidem et universorum Pater, unum etiam Verbum universorum, et Spiritus Sanctus unus et ipse est ubique. Una autem et sola est mater virgo; mihi autem placet eam vocare Ecclesiam. Lac non habuit mater haec sola, quoniam sola non fuit mulier; . . . . quae suos accersens infantulos sancto lacte, nempe Verbo infantili enutrit. . . . Verbum est omnia infanti. . . . *Comedite,* inquit, *meam carnem et hibite meum sanguinem* (*Paedagogus,* I, 6; *P.G.*, VIII, 300).

[5] " Accepit Jesus Dominus noster in manibus suis merum ab initio panem et benedixit, signavit ac sanctificavit eum in nomine Patris et in nomine Spiritus, et fregit atque distribuit." (*Hymni et Sermones,* IV, 4; La I, 416).

Finally, St. Cyril of Jerusalem explicitly affirms that the sacrament of the Eucharist is accomplished by the power of the Blessed Trinity. Before the invocation of the Trinity, he says, there is only bread and wine—nothing more. After the invocation, there is the Body and Blood of Christ[6]. The change is effected in the following way: we ask the Father to send the Spirit and it is the Holy Ghost Who causes the change of substances[7].

We note, then, a measure of progress in the development of the doctrine that links the Eucharist with the mystery of the Blessed Trinity, but side by side with this development we find repeated affirmations by the same authors of the primordial importance of the words of consecration.

St. Justin, after mentioning the prayers addressed to the Trinity, insists on the reality of the conversion of bread and wine into the Body and Blood of Christ, and to prove that there is a real change of substance he appeals to the words of Christ—*Hoc est corpus meum . . . hic est sanguis meus*[8].

St. Cyril of Jerusalem, who with St. Basil was one of the staunchest champions of the effective validity of the Epiclesis, adds these words which reveal the fundamental trend of his thought: "Since Christ Himself has said of the bread 'This is My Body', who can dare to doubt it? And since He also affirmed 'This is My Blood', will anyone dare say that it is not His Blood?"[9]

While Catholic teaching insists on the reality of the presence of Christ wrought by the transubstantiation of bread and wine into the Precious Body and Blood, and while it maintains—after long controversy—that the words of consecration alone have the power to effect that change, nevertheless we cannot dissociate ourselves from the traditional stream of thought in the Church which sees

---

[6] " Quemadmodum enim panis et vinum eucharistiae ante sanctam adorandae Trinitatis invocationem nudus panis et vinum erat, invocatione autem peracta panis fit corpus Christi et ninum sanguis Christi, ita et ejusmodi esculenta ad pompam Satanae pertinentia cum ex natura sua nuda et communia sint, invocatione daemonum profana et contaminata reddunur." (*Catecheses*, 19 (*Mystagogica*, I); *P.G.*, XXXV, 1072).

[7] " Deinde, postquam nosmetipsos per has spirituales laudes sanctificavimus, Deum benignum exoramus ut emittat Sanctum Spiritum super proposita, ut faciat panem quidem corpus Christi, vinum vero sanguinem Christi. Omnino enim quodcumque attigerit Spiritum Sanctum, id sanctificatum et transmutatum est." (*Catecheses*, 23 (*Mystag.*, 5); *P.G.*, XXXV, 1113).

[8] *Apol.*, 66; *P.G.*, VI, 428.

[9] *Catecheses*, 22 (*Mystag.*, 4), I; *P.G.*, XXXV, 1097.

an intimate link between the mysteries of the Eucharist and the Blessed Trinity.

To explain this link, it is not sufficient to appeal to the fact that every divine operation *ad extra* is common to the Three Divine Persons, because the Eucharist resembles the Incarnation in this that it is not simply a work of God *ad extra*. In the Incarnation, the Humanity of Christ is assumed by the Divine Word in such a way that it subsists in and through the Divine Personality of the Word. The term of the Incarnation is not exterior to God, it is immanent in the Word.

Likewise, in the Blessed Eucharist, the term of the changing of the substance of bread and wine is the substance of the Body and Blood of Christ. This is more than mere exteriority such as we find in the work of creation. Transubstantiation is not a fresh creation; it is a mystery of change that terminates in Christ. It is a mystery that inheres in Christ, the Incarnate Word.

In considering the Eucharist, we must not, then, limit ourselves to discovering traces of the action of the Blessed Trinity such as we can find in the work of creation. We must see the Real Presence as the centre and pivotal point of a whole new series of relations between us and the Blessed Trinity, relations which we deem to be well established in traditional Catholic thought. The existence and scope of these relations is already expressed in the words of Our Lord: "He who eats my flesh and drinks my blood *abides in me and I in him*"[10].

The Body and Blood of Christ in becoming our food give us the whole and entire Christ and give us wholly and entirely to Christ. Holy Communion effects perfect union between the human person and the Person of the Word Who gives Himself to be relished by us. The term of this sacramental union is our enjoyment of the Divinity of Christ.

By Holy Communion, the Word is present in us not merely in the same way as He is present in all things by His omnipresence; He is in us as food, as an object of spiritual enjoyment and of beatifying possession. On the other hand, He establishes us *in Him*, transforming us by grace into His own life: *in me manet*.

The Fathers understood and expressed this reciprocal indwelling in terms of more than ordinary realism. St. Hilary, after affirming

---

[10] John, VI, 57.

the reality of the presence of Christ's Body and Blood in the Eucharist, adds these words: "By eating His Body and drinking His Blood we are established in Christ and Christ in us"[11].

There are two texts of St. John Chrysostom which complement and explain each other as expressions of the saint's doctrine on the Eucharist: "He did not deem it sufficient to become man, to be buffeted and immolated; He commingles with us (*seipsum commiscet nobiscum*) and makes us His Body not only by faith but in very truth (*reipsa*)"[12].

Again, commenting on the words of the Apostle—*panis quem frangimus nonne communicatio corporis Christi est*—he points out that St. Paul was not satisfied with his explanation of the union between Christ and the Christian until he had affirmed that in Holy Communion the Christian *becomes* the Body of Christ. Let us follow in broad outline the various stages in this gradation of thought.

Why, asks St. John Chrysostom, does St. Paul use the word *communicatio* and not *participatio*? The reason is that he wished to express a more intimate degree of union. Even when he uses the word *communicatio*, which supposes a distinction of persons between him who communicates and him who receives the communication, St. Paul is at pains to attenuate this distinction, adding immediately, "We are all one bread, one body"; as if he were to say, "Why speak of communication or communion? We are the same body".

For what is the bread we eat? It is the Body of Christ. And those who communicate become the Body of Christ; not several bodies but *one* Body. Just as bread is compounded of many grains in such a way that their union obliterates their individual differences, so too with us; we are united one with the other, all united in Christ because all are nourished by the same Body"[13].

---

[11] " Nunc enim et ipsius Domini professione et fide nostra vere caro est et vere sanguis est. Et haec accepta et hausta id efficiunt ut et nos in Christo et Christus in nobis sit." (*De Trinitate*, VIII, 14; *P.L.*, X, 247).

[12] " Neque enim satis habuit hominem fieri, alapi caedi, immolari, sed seipsum commiscet nobiscum non fide tantum sed reipsa nos corpus suum constituit." (*In Matth. Homiliae*, LXXXII, 5; *P.G.*, LX, 743).

[13] " Panis quem frangimus nonne communicatio corporis Christi est? Cur non dixit participatio? Quia voluit quid amplius significare et magnam indicare conjunctionem. Non enim cum participamus tantum et sumimus, sed etiam cum conjungimur communicamus. Quemadmodum enim corpus illud Christo jungitur, *ita* et nos per panem hunc unimur. Deinde quia dixit . . . *Communicatio*

With even greater vigour of expression, St. Chrysostom thus describes our transformation in Christ: "We are the Body which we receive".

St. Cyril takes this idea of the identification of the Christian with Christ in Holy Communion and develops it by means of a comparison. Two portions of wax when melted by heat fuse together in such perfect union that they become one: *unum quid ex doubus*. Participation in the Body and Blood of Christ produces a similar unity. We are in Christ and He in us. A corruptible nature cannot be vivified in any other way than by corporeal union with the Body of Him Whose Person is Life itself, the Only Begotten Son of God[14].

Finally, we have the words of St. Leo the Great: Participation in the Body and Blood of Christ changes us into that which we eat"[15].

Reading these texts, one cannot help thinking of the analogy they afford between the Eucharist and the Incarnation. By virtue of the Hypostatic Union, the Humanity of Christ is assumed by the Word in such a way that it lives by the Life of the Word. We must say, then, that the Humanity of Christ abides *in* the Word, since it exists by the existence of the Word, and also that the Word abides *in* the Sacred Humanity.

In the Eucharist, the Christian who communicates with Christ by eating His Body and drinking His Blood is not indeed united to the Word hypostatically, since he retains his own personality distinct from the Person of the Son. But the two persons, human

---

corporis, quod autem communicat aliud est ab eo cui communicat; hanc etiam quae perva videbatur esse, differentiam sustulit. Cum dixisset enim *communicatio corporis* quaesivit rursus aliquid propinquius dicere; ideo subjunxit: Quoniam unus panis et unum corpus multi sumus. Quid enim, inquit, dico communicationem? Illud ipsum corpus sumus. Quid est enim panis? Corpus Christi. Quid autem fiunt communicantes? Corpus Christi, non corpora multa sed unum corpus. Sicut enim panis ex multis granis constans, unitus est ita ut grana nusquam appareant sed sint quidem ipsa, non manifesta autem sit illorum differentia propter conjunctionem; sic et nos et mutuo et cum Christo conjungimur. Non enim ex altero corpore hic, et altero ille nutritur, sed ex eodem ipso omnes." (*In Epistulam I ad Cor. homil.*, XXIV, 2; *P.G.*, LXIII, 200).

[14] " Ut enim si quis ceram cerae indutam igne simul liquaverit unum quid ex ambobus efficit, ita per corporis Christi et pretiosi sanguinis participationem ipse quidem in nobis, nos autem rursus in eo simul unimur. Neque enim aliter vivificari potest quod natura sua est corruptible quam si corporaliter unitum sit corpori ejus qui secundum naturam suam est vita, hoc est Unigeniti." (*In Joannem Commentarius*, X, 2; (XV, 1); *P.G.*, LXXVI, 341).

[15] *Sermones*, LXIII, 7; *P.L.*, LIV, 358.

and divine, come together in the closest union possible; by grace, their lives commingle in such a unique way that each lives in the other.

Eating the Body of Christ is the origin of a transforming process by which the person of the Christian is conformed to the Person of Christ. The consequences of this transforming union deeply affect all the Christian's relations with Christ.

Abiding in Christ, in the Word Incarnate, the Christian necessarily comes into close union with the Father and the Holy Ghost —since the three Divine Persons of the Son brings the Christian as son of God into close intimacy with the Father and gives him a share in the relations which characterize the Divine Sonship within the Trinity.

How does the Son abide in the Father? Undoubtedly it is first of all by an eternal act of self-oblation, by a total yielding up of His Person to the Father. But more than this, the Son abides in the Father by enjoying all the riches of the Father—*omnia tua mea sunt*[16]. The adopted son of God united to the Word in Holy Communion is also united to the Word in the bosom of the Father, and with the Word he, too, enjoys the riches of the Father.

The Son also abides in the Holy Ghost because with the Father He is the principle whence the Third Divine Person proceeds. But the Son is also in the Holy Ghost by an eternal inherence; and the Son rejoices in the Spirit of Love. For the Holy Ghost contains the Father and the Son from Whom He proceeds, as love holds lovers closely united in a happy embrace.

United to the Father and the Son the Christian also abides in the Holy Ghost, embraced by the Spirit of loving union who holds united all those persons—human and divine—who meet in Him. By grace the adopted child of God is connumbered with the Divine Family.

While agreeing so far, one may be inclined to object that this mutual indwelling of the Christian and the Divine Persons is already realized at Baptism when the Blessed Trinity comes into the soul and takes up Its abode there. The other sacraments intensify the bonds of this mutual indwelling by bringing the life of grace to greater perfection. Why, then, attribute this special effect to the Eucharist alone?

---

[16] John, XVII, 10.

It is in this connection that the statement of St. Thomas to which we referred at the beginning of this chapter has special application:

The Eucharist, he says, perfects and completes the other sacraments and they in their turn participate in some way in the power of the Eucharist. The other sacraments cause grace; they initiate or intensify the presence of God in the soul. The Eucharist, however, is unique in that it contains God Himself and gives God to the soul as its nourishment, so that the soul may find its enjoyment in Him.

In this enjoyment of God supernatural life reaches its climax. The most distinctive characteristic of all life, and of supernatural life more than any other, consists not in the capacity to communicate itself to others but in the immanent possession by the living being of all the good which is life itself. In other words, life is more basically *self-possession* than *self-communication*.

Just as immanent vitality expresses itself in every vital action, but nevertheless reaches its fullest expression in some specialized domain (e.g., in thought or love, in the case of human life), so the presence of God in the soul and the reciprocal indwelling of the just man and the Divine Persons which is inaugurated and increased by Baptism and the other sacraments, reaches a supreme degree of beatifying intimacy in the Blessed Eucharist.

What is true of the individual life of man is also true *a fortiori* of man's social life. To live in society is to possess life's treasure in common and to enjoy that treasure together with others.

The higher the life that is shared, the higher the happiness of the whole society. And since Christian social life is based on a participation in the society of the Divine Persons, or, rather, since our social life is closely interwoven with the life of the Divine Persons, it follows that the *summum* of happiness possible on earth consists in the reciprocal flow of life and love between the members of the human society and the Persons Who constitute the Triune society in God.

For the Divine Persons, sharing the absolute identity of the Divine Nature, are not only constituted in hierarchical relations based on the order of origins (Father—Son—Holy Ghost); not only do the Divine Persons give themselves to each other so as to abide in each other; but by the mutual gift of their Persons they live in mutual divine enjoyment of each other.

This ineffable life of the Blessed Trinity is the inaccessible apex towards greater perfection of life, especially those living beings who are endowed with the privilege of personal life.

To take one example: when a person loves, what does he seek if not the enjoyment of another person? When we love others, we wish to enjoy their presence fully, to possess them in ourselves and to be possessed by them. We wish to possess their thoughts, their sentiments, their heart and to rest in that possession. Since love is so all-embracing it is frequently exclusive of all other persons.

Love is prevented from degenerating into egoistical self-seeking and from becoming a tyrannical monopoly of another person by the realization that our enjoyment of another person is balanced by the fact that we are ourselves an object of enjoyment to the other. Possession brings but an imperfect degree of happiness; to know ourselves possessed is the summit of happiness.

An infinite love between infinite Persons is also a thing of mutual possession. It differs from all other loves in that the happiness it begets is infinite and absolute since the gift and the possession of each Person is infinitely perfect as is also the life that they share in common.

It follows from what has been said that the Eucharist by transforming the Christian in Christ bestows on him that perfection of Divine Life which consists in the personal enjoyment of God. The other sacraments conform us to Christ and enable us to live His life and in Him to come to the Father and the Holy Ghost. The Eucharist, by enabling us to enjoy a Divine Person, introduces us into the most secret mystery of life within the Blessed Trinity.

Not only does each Person in the most perfect unity (the unity of the Divine Nature) give Himself to the others and abide in them, but each eternally enjoys the infinite riches of the others. This is life in the supreme degree, infinite life eternally at rest in the perfect and mutual possession of the Three Divine Persons. In the Eucharist, God has willed to give us a sacrament wherein by a real and reciprocal possession of the Word we may have a foretaste of eternal life in God.

Our theology speaks of the effects of the Eucharist in words whose simplicity might blind us to the fullness of the mystery they express. The sacramental grace of the Blessed Eucharist, say the theological authors, is a grace of union with Christ; a grace that is food; a grace that welds together in one all those who communicate in the Body of Christ; a grace, finally, that is a foretaste of heavenly glory. Each of these terms is explained as follows:

A grace of union with Christ—real, intimate, transforming moral and affective union. If we cannot say that it is substantial and physical, this is to preclude the possibility of believing that it destroys the real distinction between the Person of Christ and the person of the Christian.

A grace that is food. Food sustains, increases and restores vital energies; it is also a source of delight. We insist on the last-mentioned effect in regard to the Eucharist because it expresses in a more positive manner the action of the sacrament which the Church describes in the antiphon: *Omne delectamentum in se habentem.* . . . Containing in itself all manner of delight.

A grace of fraternal union between Christians. In social life nothing brings men so close together as eating at the same table. What, then, must be the effect of communing in that Sacred Banquet which nourishes souls with divine charity in Person? From the early days of the Church the faithful were actually conscious of their close union based on the fact that they had communicated in the Body of Christ.

The expressions used by St. Paul—*quoniam unus panis, unum corpus, multi sumus omnes qui de uno pane participamus*[17]— occur repeatedly in the Didache Apostolorum, where we also find the prayer to the Father asking Him to unite the Church from all points of the compass, just as the seed scattered abroad on the hillside coalesces to form one bread[18]. Later, St. John Chrysostom, among others, repeats the same idea: Christians form one Body because they have eaten the same Body[19].

A grace that is a foretaste of eternal life. Let us state it in the most emphatic terms: this grace is eternal life tasted here and now in anticipation. It is a transforming union in the Person of the Word, mutual possession and mutual enjoyment of Christ and the Christian.

For if it is true to say that supreme Christian beatitude consists in the enjoyment of Christ and the enjoyment of God in Christ, we

---

[17] I Cor. X, 17.
[18] *Didache*, X, 5; F. I, 22.
[19] *In Epistulam I ad Cor. homilae*, XXIV, 2; P.G., LXIII, 200.

must add immediately that Christ too finds His delight in dwelling in the Christian soul: *Deliciae meae esse cum filiis hominum.* There is no need to strain the meaning of any text to see in the Eucharist the most perfect realization here below of this divine preference.

Christ the Eternal Word made flesh, mutiplied in His Eucharistic Presence, takes man to Himself, raises him to share in the most intimate mystery of His own personal life, and lets him share in the enjoyment of the Father and the Holy Ghost.

CONCLUSION

AMONG THE problems in sacramental theology to which a final solution has not yet been found is the question of sacramental grace. Theologians hold as certain that each sacrament produces a special grace proper to that sacrament alone and that this sacramental grace is something more than sanctifying grace. There are strong reasons to uphold these two theses.

Supposing, for example, that the sacraments produced nothing more than sanctifying grace, we should then need only two sacraments to put us in possession of the full benefits of the sacramental system—Baptism which wipes out original sin, and Penance which remits actual sin committed after Baptism. Why, then, are there seven sacraments?

Furthermore, since what is called common grace is nothing else but sanctifying grace, it would follow that a person who lived and advanced in grace without receiving any sacrament would possess the equivalent of sacramental grace. For these reasons we are compelled to admit that sacramental grace does add something to sanctifying grace.

In what does this "something" consist, this special grace which each sacrament causes as its own proper effect? Must we, with Cajetan, understand it as a right or claim to receive actual grace in view of the end proper to each sacrament? Or are we to see in sacramental grace a permanent and intrinsic reality, a certain modality of sanctifying grace to which would correspond all the actual graces of which that modality was the principle and the measure?

The trend we have followed in the course of the preceding chapters indicates the direction in which, to our mind, an answer to the problem must be sought.

Each sacrament conforms us to Christ in a special way, enabling us to reproduce in our lives some aspect of His Personal Life. This means that in addition to bestowing ordinary sanctifying grace, each sacrament also bestows a special mode of supernatural existence, a new modality of grace as distinct from other modalities as the phenomena of growth, nutrition and reproduction are distinct from the phenomenon of physical birth.

Nevertheless, it is the same life that begins at birth, that grows through various stages and that is the source of all vital activity. A similar process occurs in the supernatural life of grace, and our concluding pages will be devoted to a comprehensive survey of this phenomenon in relation to each of the sacraments.

1. *Baptism* means more than the remission of original sin. It is a true birth, endowed with all the positive reality expressed in the words "to be born", "to come to life". In the mystery of Baptism we discover much more than the beauty and wonderful charm of the first beginning of life. Baptism is an expression in time of a mystery that is eternal. There is a Person, the Son, Who is eternally begotten in God in a mystery whose eternal duration does not exhaust or diminish its eternal newness.

Baptism conforms the Christian to the mystery of the Son Who is eternally born of the Father. Through grace, the baptised soul shares in the characteristics of the eternal generation—resemblance to the Father, newness of life, vocation to give witness everywhere and at all times to the splendour of the Divine Life which surges up from the bosom of the Father.

Baptism makes the adopted son of God a living example of all that characterizes the eternal generation and the temporal mission of the Son.

2. Life, however, is not only a dawn of great promise. It reaches fulfilment in a warm midday of fruitfulness. The Son of God, radiant with the splendour of the Father, is charged with accomplishing a programme of universal redemption. His is an immense task. He is sent on earth to reveal Him from Whom He is eternally born. He is charged with rebuilding the world in grace, making a new world and peopling it with a new generation of men.

Christians are called to conformity with Christ, the Artisan of this vast scheme. Become another Christ by his supernatural birth at Baptism, the Christian must also share with Christ in His redemptive campaign.

Confirmation is not only an arming for combat against the enemies of the Church; it confers the strength required for the reconstruction of the world. The Christian cannot undertake, much less accomplish, this heroic task unless the gift of the Holy Ghost conforms him to Christ the Builder of His Church.

3. The task is one of rebuilding what had collapsed. It entails the establishment of an order in which justice and mercy are closely interwoven. The new world cannot rise from earth and tend upwards towards God except by the constant reparation of faults and errors.

The sacrament of *Penance* was specially instituted for this work of re-building; it is a sacrament which achieves the ends of divine justice by the administration of divine pardon.

In this sacrament both priest and penitent are conformed to the Christ Whose whole Life on earth was an exercise of divine goodness and mercy, Who repeated on so many occasions the words, "Thy sins are forgiven thee". The penitent, by accusing himself with contrite heart and by accepting the penance laid on him in satisfaction for sin, is thereby restored to union with Christ.

Undoubtedly, the Lord of all grace could not destroy sin in Himself since sin had no place in Him. But He destroyed the evil that reigned in the world about Him and He restored the order of justice by the triumph of His mercy among sinners. His whole life was a combat against sin and He emerged from the struggle victorious through love.

The penitent resembles his Master in that he, like Christ, triumphs over sin by love, since his contrition, as an act of detestation of sin, includes an act of the love of God and a love of the order of divine justice. Satisfaction is also an expression of one's will to restore by love the order that was destroyed by sin.

Thus by his personal acts, which constitute the matter of the sacrament of Penance, the sinner touched by grace truly unites himself to Christ in restoring justice through an act of love. That act is both one of love of God and of mercy towards his own soul; the justice that is restored is the re-establishment of right order, and order consists in union with God.

Penance, we are well aware, is not to be compared to a second-hand market; it is not a way of obtaining a bargain in second-hand grace. The sacrament was instituted to bring a sinful world into harmony with the infinity of divine mercy.

Each Person in the Blessed Trinity dispenses the divine mercy according to the special attributes which characterize Him as a distinct Person: The Father, as the primal source of all mercy, shows mercy by sending His Son; the Son, Architect of the scheme of divine goodness of which He is the eternal and living expression; finally, the sinner, converted by grace, and the Son through Whom all mercy and justice is accomplished, and the Father to Whom the sinner returns reconciled—all meet and are made one in abiding union in the Holy Ghost.

This supernatural life, even in repairing the loss of grace, achieves a wonderful consecration of the whole man, raising him up again to share in the splendour of the first of all mysteries, the mystery of the Blessed Trinity.

4. But our Divine Life would not be in real continuity with the source from which it springs did it not share the limitless fecundity of that divine source. The sacraments of *Matrimony* and *Holy Orders,* complementary to each other in the communication of Divine Life on earth, ensure the mystery of perpetual fecundity within the Church.

Matrimony sanctifies and gives supernatural value to the acts of husband and wife with a view to the procreation of children, who will in their turn become a new generation of children of God.

By its conformity with the union existing between Christ and the Church, and by its participation in that union, Christian marriage consecrates wedded life to that Love which is eternally the Father, eternally the Son, eternally the Spirit of Divine Family.

For both husband and wife, Matrimony opens up the perspective of a life together in which the inner Life of the Blessed Trinity is visibly reflected.

5. *Holy Orders,* the sacrament of spiritual paternity, is the source of a stream of grace that never ceases to flow over the world, vitalizing the souls of men and even giving supernatural value to material things. By it the work of carnal generation is crowned by the supernatural generation of sons of God.

6. Life, all life, finally ends in the complete and total sacrifice of itself. The gift of self to the utmost limit of all giving—this is the secret of life's apotheosis.   It is a mystery of enchanting beauty, a mystery that is endlessly reflected on earth—in the soft beauty of autumn when branches that have borne a rich panoply of

blossom and fruit are finally gilt by death with a tender blaze of glory.

There is a beauty immeasurably more sublime in the autumn of human lives that end in the heroism of total self-oblation for the good of society and of the whole world. Here is the crowning splendour of a life that never turns back, a life that concentrates all its force in one supreme sacrifice, in that last breath which for ever consecrates the self-oblation of a lifetime.

There is such lofty grandeur linked with such lowly weakness in the death of a Christian. It is an offering that goes to the ultimate limit of oblation, and at the moment of death life receives its final and inalterable determination. At the moment when his nature is on the brink of dissolution, man sums up his whole life and gives final expression to the meaning of his life in a single word, his last word of acceptance and resignation.

The sacrament of *Extreme Unction* reconciles these extremes of grandeur and weakness, and consecrates man's total offering of Himself on the Cross. In the death-offering of Christ there was the blending of the utter weakness of a nature that cried out, "Father, if it be possible, let this chalice pass from me", with the glorious consummation expressed in the words, "Father, into Thy hands I commend my spirit".

The dying Christian is conformed to that death by which a Divine Person, immortal in His divine Nature, found in His human nature the means of offering Himself to the very end after the manner of men. On the Cross it is the Person of the Word Who offers Himself, but He makes His offering in accordance with the new mode of being which He assumed in time by becoming incarnate.

Hence the sacrament of Extreme Unction conforms the Christian to the Person of the Word, Who through dying in His Humanity none the less performs a divine action. This divine act of the Incarnate Word offering Himself to the Father in the Holy Ghost is an act which the Divine Persons elicit eternally within the Trinity.

Not that the Divine Persons die for each other—God cannot die in Himself—but they give themselves to each other with all the infinity of being with which each is personally identified. They give themselves totally and eternally. Since the Word became Man it was fitting that He should give Himself to the Father in the most complete and absolute way possible for man—by dying.

The sacrament of the dying is, then, a sacrament of sublime consecration. It seizes on man in the extremity of human weakness, elevates his weakness to the grandeur of limitless self-oblation, and thereby conforms him to God the Son Who found in death the secret of offering Himself in a new way to the Father.

7. Finally, in the life of the higher living creatures, according as they develop and communicate their life to others and come to their final dissolution, there is an intrinsic element of enjoyment. Supernatural life, since it is life at its most perfect, is also characterized by supreme delight. Immanent activity, more than any other kind of activity, expresses itself in the possession and enjoyment of the intrinsic values of life itself.

To regard life exclusively and above all else as a thing of struggle and effort is to emphasize only one aspect, and that its more external aspect; it is to ignore the full richness of life in its deepest reality. Life is indeed a thing of sorrow while it is in the painful stages of parturition.

Though the possession of knowledge is a source of delight and contentment, the acquisition of knowledge can be a painful process; and although the gift of self in love leads to real and deep happiness (*Beatius*), it presupposes the painful mortification of the many roots of egoism. But once the goal of striving has been attained, life blossoms into abundance of delight.

Life is the possession and enjoyment of its own intrinsic good. Shall we be surprised that there is a sacrament whose most sublime rôle is to bring souls to rest in the enjoyment of Divine Life?

This is the deep reality underlying the *Blessed Eucharist,* the sacrament which enables us to possess and enjoy Life in its divine plenitude, in the Person of Jesus Christ. It is for this reason that the Eucharist is called the pledge and the foretaste of the life of Heaven.

Even before our entry into eternal rest, the Eucharist gives us possession of the living God as the object of our delight. In this sacrament our souls feed on the living God and draw draughts of delight from the same living God.

It is to be noted that in giving Himself to us in Holy Communion as our joy and our soul's contentment, Jesus Christ expresses the divine manner in which the Persons communicate with each other within the Trinity, by the total giving of self and by the reciprocal indwelling of the Three Divine Persons. Not only do the Divine Persons give themselves totally and without reserve, not only does each offer the full riches of His Personality, but they dwell in each other eternally.

The "abide in me and I in you" which is so perfectly realized in the Blessed Eucharist, is an expression of that divine and unique manner of self-donation by which one person dwells in another. Such indwelling is proper to God alone, but man is called to participate in it by abiding in Christ.

By permitting man to share in the mystery of the intercommunion of the Divine Persons in the Blessed Trinity, the Blessed Eucharist marks the summit of the whole sacramental system. In Holy Communion our Divine Life rejoins the divine source from which it issued, to abide there in intimate union.

From all that has preceded, we see how the sacraments signify and effect an ever closer conformity between the Christian and Christ, between the baptized person and the Person of the Word. Necessarily, then, they mark various stages of the development of Divine Life in us.

Man's life, especially his Divine Life, which pledges him to rise to an even greater degree of intimacy with God, is not and cannot be considered an inert reality, like a stagnant mass of water undisturbed by any current. Life, supernatural life above all, grows and develops under many aspects which all reflect the creature's participation in the infinite mystery of life in God.

Divine Life, in its source and in its term, is infinitely perfect; it exists as eternal plenitude of life without possibility of increase or further perfection. But Divine Life, communicated to man by grace, would not be a truly divine gift, would not be truly life, if it did not express itself under a multiplicity of forms as a vital energy ever seeking new fields of conquest.

Furthermore, to become "deiform" it does not suffice that a man possess a share in the Life of God. He must also live and act after the manner of the Divine Persons. It is the function of the sacraments to help him to do this.

Throughout the complexity of his existence here below, the sacraments conform the adopted son of God to the Person of the eternally begotten Son of the Father. They plunge the Christian deeper and deeper into the eneffable stream of the divine relations within the Trinity where Person offers to Person the infinite gift of the Absolute Good.

www.ingramcontent.com/pod-product-compliance
Lightning Source LLC
Chambersburg PA
CBHW021642120626
46545CB00002B/669